GLORIA CHUKWUMA

Crystallization-Study
of
Genesis

Volume One

Witness Lee

The
Holy
Word
for
Morning
Revival

Living Stream Ministry

Anaheim, CA • www.lsm.org

First Edition, July 2013.

ISBN 978-0-7363-6595-6

Published by

Living Stream Ministry
2431 W. La Palma Ave., Anaheim, CA 92801 U.S.A.
P. O. Box 2121, Anaheim, CA 92814 U.S.A.

Printed in the United States of America

13 14 15 16 / 5 4 3 2 1

2013 Summer Training

CRYSTALLIZATION-STUDY OF GENESIS

Contents

Preface

1. This book is intended as an aid to believers in developing a daily time of morning revival with the Lord in His word. At the same time, it provides a limited review of the summer training held July 1-6, 2013, in Anaheim, California, on the "Crystallization-study of Genesis." Through intimate contact with the Lord in His word, the believers can be constituted with life and truth and thereby equipped to prophesy in the meetings of the church unto the building up of the Body of Christ.

2. The book is divided into weeks. One training message is covered per week. Each week presents first the message outline, followed by six daily portions, a hymn, and then some space for writing. The training outline has been divided into days, corresponding to the six daily portions. Each daily portion covers certain points and begins with a section entitled "Morning Nourishment." This section contains selected verses and a short reading that can provide rich spiritual nourishment through intimate fellowship with the Lord. The "Morning Nourishment" is followed by a section entitled "Today's Reading," a longer portion of ministry related to the day's main points. Each day's portion concludes with a short list of references for further reading and some space for the saints to make notes concerning their spiritual inspiration, enlightenment, and enjoyment to serve as a reminder of what they have received of the Lord that day.

3. The space provided at the end of each week is for composing a short prophecy. This prophecy can be composed by considering all of our daily notes, the "harvest" of our inspirations during the week, and preparing a main point with some sub-points to be spoken in the church meetings for the organic building up of the Body of Christ.

4. Following the last week in this volume, we have provided reading schedules for both the Old and New Testaments in the Recovery Version with footnotes. These schedules are arranged so that one can read through both the Old and

New Testaments of the Recovery Version with footnotes in two years.

5. As a practical aid to the saints' feeding on the Word throughout the day, we have provided verse cards at the end of the volume, which correspond to each day's Scripture reading. These may be cut out and carried along as a source of spiritual enlightenment and nourishment in the saints' daily lives.

6. The content of this book is taken primarily from *Crystallization-study Outlines: Genesis (1)*, the text and footnotes of the Recovery Version of the Bible, selections from the writings of Witness Lee and Watchman Nee, and *Hymns*, all of which are published by Living Stream Ministry.

7. *Crystallization-study Outlines: Genesis (1)* was compiled by Living Stream Ministry from the writings of Witness Lee and Watchman Nee. The outlines, footnotes, and cross-references in the Recovery Version of the Bible are by Witness Lee. Unless otherwise noted, the references cited in this publication are by Witness Lee.

8. For the sake of space, references to *The Collected Works of Watchman Nee* and *The Collected Works of Witness Lee* are abbreviated to *CWWN* and *CWWL*, respectively.

CRYSTALLIZATION-STUDY OF GENESIS

Banners:

God's intention in creating man
in His image and according to His likeness
is that man would receive Him as life
and express Him in His attributes,
and God's intention in giving man dominion
is to subdue His enemy, recover the earth,
and exercise His authority over the earth.

The tree of life as the center
of God's eternal economy typifies Christ,
the embodiment of the Triune God,
to be life and the life supply
to the tripartite man as a vessel
for the corporate expression of God—
this is the central thought of God.

As God's people love God and spend time
to fellowship with Him in His word,
God infuses them with His divine element,
making them one with Him as His spouse,
the same as He is in life, nature, and expression.

The seed of the woman is the individual Christ—
the One who bruised the serpent
through His death on the cross—
and also the corporate Christ—the man-child,
including Christ as the Head
and the overcoming believers as the Body—
who will defeat God's enemy
and bring in His kingdom so that
His eternal purpose might be accomplished.

The Central Thought of God

Scripture Reading: Gen. 1:26; 2:7-10, 18-25; Rev. 22:1-2; 21:2, 9-10, 18-21

Day 1 I. God's desire and purpose is to have a corporate man to express Him in His image and to represent Him with His authority; in order for man to express God and represent God, he must have God as his life, signified by the tree of life (Gen. 1:26; 2:8-9; Rom. 8:28-29; 2 Cor. 3:16-18; Rom. 5:10, 17, 21; 16:20).

Day 2 II. The revelation concerning the garden of Eden, as the beginning of the divine revelation in the Holy Scriptures, and the revelation concerning the New Jerusalem, as the ending of the divine revelation in the Holy Scriptures, reflect each other; what is revealed in these two parts of the Scriptures is the central thought of God, the central line of the divine revelation, and a controlling principle of the interpreting and understanding of the Holy Scriptures:

   A. Genesis 1 and 2 are the blueprint of God's organic architectural plan to have His divine building (Heb. 11:10; 1 Cor. 3:9).

   B. Genesis 3 through Revelation 20 are the building process.

   C. Revelation 21 and 22 are the photograph of the finished building, the corporate expression of the Triune God.

Day 3 III. Genesis 1—2 and Revelation 21—22 both contain four organic items, showing the procedures God takes to fulfill His purpose:

   A. The tree of life as the center of God's eternal economy typifies Christ, the embodiment of the Triune God, to be life and the life supply to the tripartite man as a vessel for the corporate

expression of God—this is the central thought of
God (Gen. 2:7-9; Rev. 22:2; cf. Gen. 3:24; Ezek.
1:28; 1 Cor. 1:30; Eph. 3:10; Rev. 21:19-20):

1. "In Him was life, and the life was the light of
   men. And the light shines in the darkness,
   and the darkness did not overcome it" (John
   1:4-5).
2. "I am...the life" (14:6; cf. 15:5).
3. "I have come that they may have life and
   may have it abundantly" (10:10b).
4. "Truly, truly, I say to you, Unless the grain
   of wheat falls into the ground and dies, it
   abides alone; but if it dies, it bears much
   fruit" (12:24).
5. "If you knew the gift of God and who it is
   who says to you, Give Me a drink, you would
   have asked Him, and He would have given
   you living water...The water that I will give
   him will become in him a fountain of water
   springing up into eternal life" (4:10, 14).
6. "I am the bread of life...He who eats Me, he
   also shall live because of Me...It is the
   Spirit who gives life; the flesh profits nothing; the words which I have spoken to you
   are spirit and are life" (6:35, 57, 63).
7. "The last Adam became a life-giving Spirit"
   (1 Cor. 15:45b).
8. "The law of the Spirit of life has freed me
   in Christ Jesus from the law of sin and of
   death" (Rom. 8:2).
9. "If Christ is in you, though the body is dead
   because of sin, the spirit is life because of
   righteousness" (v. 10).
10. "The mind set on the flesh is death, but the
    mind set on the spirit is life and peace" (v. 6;
    cf. 1 Cor. 6:17).
11. "If the Spirit of the One who raised Jesus
    from the dead dwells in you, He who raised
    Christ from the dead will also give life to

your mortal bodies through His Spirit who indwells you" (Rom. 8:11).

12. "Blessed are those who wash their robes that they may have right to the tree of life and may enter by the gates into the city" (Rev. 22:14; cf. Psa. 51:2, 7, 10, 12).

13. "To him who overcomes, to him I will give to eat of the tree of life, which is in the Paradise of God" (Rev. 2:7; cf. John 6:57, 63; Jer. 15:16; John 15:1, 5, 7; 8:31).

14. "[God] has also made us sufficient as ministers of a new covenant, ministers not of the letter but of the Spirit; for the letter kills, but the Spirit gives life" (2 Cor. 3:6, cf. 8-9; 5:20).

15. "If anyone sees his brother sinning a sin not unto death, he shall ask and he will give life to him" (1 John 5:16).

Day 4

B. The river flowing to reach the four directions of the earth signifies the river of water of life as the abundance of life in its flow, flowing out of the unique God as the source and center to reach man in every direction (Gen. 2:10):

1. The river of water of life proceeding out of the throne of God and of the Lamb depicts how the Triune God—God, the Lamb, and the Spirit, who is symbolized by the water of life—dispenses Himself to His redeemed under His headship (Rev. 22:1).

2. That the river of water of life proceeds "in the middle of its street" (v. 1), which is pure gold (21:21), signifies that the divine life flows in the divine nature as the unique way for the daily life of God's redeemed people (2 Pet. 1:4; John 4:24; 1 John 4:8, 16; 1:5).

3. The fellowship of the eternal life (v. 3) is the flow of the eternal life within all the believers and is depicted by the flow of the water of life in the New Jerusalem (Rev. 22:1).

4. The following verses show how we must enjoy the flowing Triune God—Jer. 2:13; Psa. 36:8-9; John 7:37-39; Exo. 17:6; Num. 20:7-8; 1 Cor. 12:3b, 13; Ezek. 47:1-9.

Day 5

C. The flow of the river issues in three precious materials: gold, bdellium, and onyx stone (Gen. 2:10-12):

1. These materials typify the Triune God as the basic elements of the structure of God's eternal building; the New Jerusalem is constructed of these three categories of materials (Rev. 21:18-21):

   a. Gold typifies God the Father with His divine nature, which man may partake of through God's calling, as the base of God's eternal building (2 Pet. 1:3-4).

   b. Bdellium, a pearl-like material produced from the resin of a tree, typifies the produce of God the Son in His redeeming and life-releasing death and His life-dispensing resurrection as the entry into God's eternal building (John 19:34; 12:24; 1 Pet. 1:3; Rev. 21:21).

   c. Onyx, a precious stone, typifies the produce of God the Spirit with His transforming work for the building up of God's eternal building (2 Cor. 3:18).

2. The flowing of the divine life in man brings the divine nature into man (2 Pet. 1:4), regenerates man (1 Pet. 1:3), and transforms man into the glorious image of Christ (2 Cor. 3:18); thus, the man who was created of dust (Gen. 2:7) becomes transformed precious materials for God's building, which will consummate in the New Jerusalem.

3. By our transformation in life, we are becoming gold, silver, and precious stones for God's building (1 Cor. 3:12):

   a. In order to build with these materials,

we ourselves must be constituted with them; we need the growth in the nature of God the Father, the redemption of God the Son, and the transformation of God the Spirit; this growth makes us gold, silver, and precious stones for God's building (vv. 12, 16-17).

b. Through our eating of Christ, along with our spiritual digestion, assimilation, and metabolism, Christ becomes us, and we become Him; then we become the precious materials for God's building (John 6:57; Eph. 3:17; Gal. 4:19).

4. God's eternal goal is the building—the temple built with precious materials on Christ as the unique foundation (1 Cor. 3:11-12, 16-17):

a. The growth in the divine life produces materials for the building of God's habitation; this habitation, the church, is the increase, the enlargement, of the unlimited Christ (Eph. 2:21-22; John 3:29-34).

b. First, we have the farm for the growth in life; then we have the building for God's eternal purpose (1 Cor. 3:9; Matt. 16:18; Eph. 2:20-22; 4:16).

5. The actual building of the church as the house of God is by the growth in life of the believers (1 Cor. 3:6-7, 16-17; Eph. 2:20-21; 1 Pet. 2:2-5):

a. True building is the growth in life; the extent to which we have been built up is the extent to which we have grown.

b. In order to have the genuine building, we need to grow by having ourselves reduced and by having Christ increased within us (Matt. 16:24; Eph. 3:17).

Day 6   D. The final step of God's procedure in fulfilling His purpose is to work Himself into man to make man His counterpart, or complement (Gen. 2:18-25; Rev. 21:2, 9-10):

1. In order to produce a complement for Himself, God first became a man, as typified by God's creation of Adam (John 1:14; Rom. 5:14).
2. Adam's deep sleep for the producing of Eve as his wife typifies Christ's death on the cross for the producing of the church as His counterpart (Eph. 5:25-27).
3. The rib taken from Adam's opened side typifies the unbreakable, indestructible, eternal life of Christ, which flowed out of His pierced side to impart life to His believers for the building up of the church as His complement (Heb. 7:16; John 19:34).
4. Genesis 2:22 does not say that Eve was created but that she was built; the building of Eve with the rib taken from Adam's side typifies the building of the church with the resurrection life released from Christ through His death on the cross and imparted into His believers in His resurrection (John 12:24; 1 Pet. 1:3).
5. Through such a process God in Christ has been wrought into man with His life and nature so that man can be the same as God in life and nature in order to match Him as His complement, His bride, His wife (Rev. 21:2, 9-10).
6. The church as the real Eve is the totality of Christ in all His believers; only that which comes out of Christ with His resurrection life can be His complement and counterpart, the Body of Christ (1 Cor. 12:12; Eph. 5:28-30).
7. At the end of the Bible is a city, New Jerusalem, the ultimate and eternal woman, the corporate bride, the wife of the Lamb, built

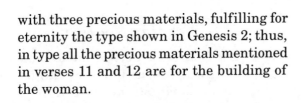

with three precious materials, fulfilling for eternity the type shown in Genesis 2; thus, in type all the precious materials mentioned in verses 11 and 12 are for the building of the woman.

Morning Nourishment

Gen. **And God said, Let Us make man in Our image,**
1:26 **according to Our likeness; and let them have do-**
minion...over all the earth...
2:9 **And out of the ground Jehovah God caused to**
grow every tree that is pleasant to the sight and
good for food, as well as the tree of life in the
middle of the garden and the tree of the knowledge
of good and evil.

God's desire and purpose are to have a corporate man to
express Him in His image and to represent Him with His
authority. Now we must ask a question: how can man express
God in His image and represent Him with His authority? (*Life-
study of Genesis,* p. 117)

After man was created, on the one hand, God rested, but on
the other hand, God's work was not completed because man did
not yet have the divine life. Up to that point, man had the form
and the appearance of God but not the life and nature, the substance, of God. In Genesis 1 there are the created lives in different degrees, but in Genesis 2 there is the unique and highest
life, the divine life, the uncreated life, signified by the tree
of life. Adam was made as the highest life among the created
lives, but he did not have the divine life at the time of creation.
God's intention was that Adam would take God as his life.
Without the divine life being accepted, received, realized, and
experienced by man, man can never be the expression and representative of God. (*The Central Thought of God,* p. 26)

Today's Reading

Although the record of creation in Genesis 1 reveals God's
purpose in creating man, it does not show us the way to fulfill
this purpose. Therefore, we need the second record [of creation
in Genesis 2] to reveal the way, the procedure, God takes to fulfill
His purpose.

God is going to accomplish His purpose by means of His own
life....If we are going to express God, we need the life of God. If

we have the life of God, we will express Him spontaneously and unconsciously. Once we have His life, we will express His image. Life is the way to fulfill God's purpose. This life is not our natural life, but the divine and eternal life of God.

Authority is also related to life....The more life you have, the more authority you have....Your age assigns you the authority. In order to represent God with His authority, we need His life.

Man was created in the image of God, but he was like a photograph showing something of God without having the life of God. Although man was in the image of God, he did not have the life of God. God intended that man should partake of the life indicated by the tree of life.

Genesis 1 reveals God's eternal purpose, which is to express Himself through man and to exercise His dominion with man. Man was created to express God and to represent God....Although God has a purpose, He must have a means of fulfilling it. What is God's divine way of accomplishing His purpose? As we have seen, His way is life. God desires to come into us as life. In order to accomplish His purpose, God wants to come into man to be man's life and life supply. Furthermore, Genesis 2 reveals that God's procedure involves three steps. The first step was for God to create man as a vessel to contain Him as life. Since man was made as a vessel to contain God, man can live by Him, express Him, and represent Him. As the second step, God placed man in front of the tree of life....In placing man before the tree of life, God was indicating that He wanted man to take Him into his being that he might be transformed into the precious materials for the building up of the church.

The first step was to make the vessel, the second was to put this vessel in front of the tree of life, and the third is to work God into man as life. (*Life-study of Genesis,* pp. 117-120, 215-216)

Further Reading: The Vision of God's Building, ch. 1; *Life-study of Genesis,* msgs. 6-8, 10; *The Central Thought of God,* ch. 3; *The Central Line of the Divine Revelation,* msgs. 5-6

Enlightenment and inspiration: _____

_____

_____

_____

Morning Nourishment

Gen.   ...Jehovah God built the rib, which He had taken from
2:22   the man, into a woman and brought her to the man.
Rev.   And the Spirit and the bride say, Come! And let him
22:17 who hears say, Come! And let him who is thirsty
       come; let him who wills take the water of life freely.

The revelation concerning the garden of Eden, as the beginning of the divine revelation in the Holy Scriptures, and the revelation concerning the New Jerusalem, as the ending of the
divine revelation in the Holy Scriptures, reflect each other. Both
contain four things: (1) the tree of life as the center of God's eternal economy (Gen. 2:9; Rev. 22:2), (2) the river flowing to reach
the four directions of the earth (Gen. 2:10; Rev. 22:1), (3) three
kinds of precious materials (Gen. 2:11-12; Rev. 21:11-14, 18-21),
and (4) a couple (Gen. 2:18-25; Rev. 21:9-10; 22:17). What is
revealed in these two parts of the Scriptures is the central line of
the divine revelation of the entire Holy Scriptures and should be
a controlling principle of the interpreting and understanding of
the Holy Scriptures. (Gen. 2:25, footnote 1)

Today's Reading

Genesis 1 and 2 are like the blueprint in the beginning of
a manual of building instructions. Revelation 21 and 22 are like a
photo of the finished structure inserted at the end of the manual.
First we look at the blueprint; then we read the building instructions and go to work; finally, at the end, we attain the finished
structure, similar in every detail to the photo in the manual. The
Scriptures are such an instruction book regarding God's building.
At the beginning there is the blueprint, and at the end there is the
completion according to the initial concept.

We must spend much time in the detailed instructions of this
"manual." But first we must be deeply impressed that we are a
vessel made with a spirit, an inner recipient to receive God. We
must learn how to exercise our spirit continually to contact and
receive God. Next we must realize that God in Christ by the
Spirit is the tree of life, the real food for us to eat and enjoy. As we

enjoy Christ in such a way, we will have the flowing of the living water within us, and by this flowing we will be transformed from clay into precious materials. Then as transformed materials we must be built up with others. We cannot be independent, precious Christians. We must learn to be related with others and very dependent. Finally, such a building will be the bride on this earth, the bride which will satisfy Christ.

The corporate man whom God is after is not only His expression and representative but also the bride to satisfy the Bridegroom. However, it is only when we are enjoying Christ as our food that we may be transformed, and it is only as we are being transformed that we may be built up with others, and it is only as we are built up with others that Christ will have full satisfaction with us. We will be the expression and representative of God as well as the bride of Christ.

We all know that in ourselves, by ourselves, and with ourselves—in our natural life—we can never be one with others. Every natural man is a peculiar man, a separate man. A husband in his natural state is not one with his wife. Although we may be in the closest relationship on earth as a husband and wife, we are individually peculiar and naturally divided. It is impossible in such a state to be one. Our natural life must be swallowed up by Christ. We must learn how to contact and feed on Christ in our spirit. We must learn how to deny our self, rejecting our natural life, and live by Christ. Then the Lord will flow within, transforming us from clay into precious stone. As we are united, related, and built up with others, God's goal will be attained.

We must see a recovery of such a testimony, a group of people who practice these things, giving all the honor and glory to the ascended Head because they are His Body on this earth. Then there will be a bride on this earth to express God and to satisfy Christ. (*The Vision of God's Building*, pp. 31-33)

Further Reading: The Vision of God's Building, ch. 2; *The Triune God's Revelation and His Move*, msg. 7; *The God-men*, ch. 4

Enlightenment and inspiration: _____

_____

_____

_____

Morning Nourishment

John **Jesus said..., I am the way and the reality and the**
14:6 **life; no one comes to the Father except through Me.**
15:1 **I am the true vine, and My Father is the husbandman.**
Rev. **Blessed are those who wash their robes that they**
22:14 **may have right to the tree of life and may enter by**
the gates into the city.

The revelation concerning the garden of Eden, as the beginning of the divine revelation in the Holy Scriptures, contains four matters (Gen. 2:8-14, 18-24). First, there is the tree of life as the center of God's eternal economy (v. 9a). Second, [there is] a river flowing into four heads to reach the four directions of the earth [vv. 10-14]. Third, at the flow of the river are three kinds of precious materials: gold, pearl, and onyx (vv. 11-12). Here these materials are scattered and not yet builded together. Fourth, there is a couple, signifying Christ and the church (vv. 18-24; Eph. 5:22-29, 32). The wife came out of the husband (signifying Christ) as a part (a rib, signifying the resurrection life of Christ) of him taken out of him in his sleep (signifying the death of Christ) by God, which part God built into a woman (signifying the church)—Gen. 2:21-22a. Then God brought the woman to the man and made her one flesh with him as her husband to be his counterpart as his increase and expression (vv. 22b-24; John 3:29a, 30; Eph. 1:23). (*The God-men*, pp. 62-63)

Today's Reading

The revelation concerning the New Jerusalem, as the ending of the divine revelation in the Holy Scriptures, also contains four matters (Rev. 21:1—22:2). First, there is the tree of life as the center of God's eternal economy (22:2). Second, according to 22:1 a river of water of life flows to reach the four directions of the earth (cf. 21:13). Third, there are three kinds of precious materials: gold, pearls, and precious stones. These materials are built together into a city, the city of New Jerusalem, by the processed and consummated Triune God (21:18-21). Fourth, the entire city is a couple. The processed and consummated redeeming Triune God in Christ is the Husband. The chosen and redeemed people

of the redeeming Triune God are the wife, produced by the processed and consummated Triune God through Christ's death and
resurrection with the divine life of the redeeming God as the element to be His counterpart as His enlargement and expression
in eternity (vv. 2, 9; Eph. 1:23; 3:19). (*The God-men*, p. 63)

As a result of the fall, Satan as the tree of knowledge came into
man's flesh. As a result of our believing in Christ, God as the tree
of life came into our spirit. Therefore, the two trees that were once
in the garden outside of man are now within us, one in our flesh
and the other in our spirit....Paul said in his flesh nothing good
dwells, only sin [Rom. 7]. Sin is actually the evil nature of Satan. To
say that sin dwells in our flesh means that Satan, the evil one, is
in our flesh. Romans 8:16, a verse which proves that God is in us,
says that the Spirit of God witnesses with our spirit. Thus, every
genuine Christian is a miniature garden of Eden. The mind of
your soul represents your self, sin in your flesh represents Satan,
and the Spirit in your spirit represents God. As in the garden of
Eden, the three parties form a triangular situation within us.

The seed of this triangular situation was sown in Genesis 2, and
the growth of the seed is found in Romans 8, where we see the out-
crop of the two trees. Romans 8:6 says that the mind set on the
flesh is death and that the mind set on the spirit is life and peace.
In Genesis 2 the two trees were objective; in Romans 8 they are
subjective....In the past I expected to uproot the tree of knowledge
in my flesh, but the more I dealt with it, the more it remained
within me. Eventually I discovered Romans 8. I saw that there is
another tree abiding in my spirit. Thus, in Romans 8 we find a
present-day garden of Eden. Romans 8:2 mentions the law of the
Spirit of life, which sets us free from the law of sin and death.
Therefore, in Romans 8 we have two laws—the law of life and the law
of death. These two laws are the two principles of the two trees in our
subjective experience. (*Life-study of Genesis*, pp. 177-178)

*Further Reading: The God-men, ch. 4; Life-study of Genesis, msgs. 11,
13-14*

Enlightenment and inspiration: _____
_____
_____
_____

Morning Nourishment

Gen. **And a river went forth from Eden to water the**
2:10 **garden, and from there it divided and became four**
branches.

Rev. **And he showed me a river of water of life, bright as**
22:1 **crystal, proceeding out of the throne of God and of**
the Lamb in the middle of its street.

Along with the tree there is a river (Gen. 2:10). Since the tree is a tree of life, the river must also be related to life. At the end of the Bible we also see a river of life flowing and a tree of life growing (Rev. 22:1-2). At the beginning and the end of the Bible we find the tree of life and a river flowing with living water. In the Scriptures the concept of the river is also crucial. When the Scripture mentions man, both in the beginning and at the end, it also mentions the river. For man to receive God as life, to enjoy the fatness of God, to quench thirst, to be watered, to grow, and to rejoice, all depends on the river. (*Life-study of Genesis*, pp. 141-142)

Today's Reading

The river [in Genesis 2:10] signifies the river of water of life, along which the tree of life grows (Rev. 22:1-2 and footnotes 1^2, 1^3, and 2^1). This river quenched man's thirst and watered the garden that life might grow. At the beginning and the end of the Bible there are the tree of life and the river flowing with living water.

The river going forth from Eden signifies the river of water of life flowing forth from God (Rev. 22:1), indicating that God is the source of the living water for man to drink (cf. John 4:10; 7:37). (Gen. 2:10, footnotes 1 and 2)

The throne of God and of the Lamb [in Revelation 22:1], showing that there is one throne for both God and the Lamb, indicates that God and the Lamb are one—the Lamb-God, the redeeming God, God the Redeemer. In eternity the very God who sits on the throne is our redeeming God, from whose throne proceeds the river of water of life for our supply and satisfaction. This depicts how the Triune God—God, the Lamb, and the Spirit, who is symbolized by the water of life—dispenses

Himself to His redeemed under His headship (implied in the authority of the throne) for eternity. (Rev. 22:1, footnote 5)

The street of the holy city is pure gold (Rev. 21:21). Gold symbolizes the divine nature. That the river of water of life proceeds "in the middle of its street" signifies that the divine life flows in the divine nature as the unique way for the daily life of God's redeemed people. Where the divine life flows, there the divine nature is as the holy way by which God's people walk; and where the holy way of the divine nature is, there the divine life is flowing. The divine life and the divine nature as the holy way always go together. Thus, God's river of water of life is available along this divine way, and we enjoy the river by walking in this way of life. (Rev. 22:1, footnote 6)

The Greek word [for *fellowship*] means *joint participation, common participation.* Fellowship is the issue of the eternal life and is actually the flow of the eternal life within all the believers, who have received and possess the divine life. It is illustrated by the flow of the water of life in the New Jerusalem (Rev. 22:1). All genuine believers are in this fellowship (Acts 2:42). It is carried on by the Spirit in our regenerated spirit. Hence, it is called "the fellowship of the Holy Spirit" (2 Cor. 13:14) and "fellowship of [our] spirit" (Phil. 2:1). It is in this fellowship of the eternal life that we, the believers, participate in all that the Father and the Son are and have done for us; that is, we enjoy the love of the Father and the grace of the Son by virtue of the fellowship of the Spirit (2 Cor. 13:14). Such a fellowship was first the apostles' portion in their enjoyment of the Father and the Son through the Spirit. Hence, in Acts 2:42 it is called "the fellowship of the apostles," and in 1 John 1:3 "our [the apostles'] fellowship," a fellowship with the Father and with His Son Jesus Christ. It is a divine mystery. This mysterious fellowship of the eternal life should be considered the subject of this Epistle. (1 John 1:3, footnote 3)

Further Reading: Life-study of Genesis, msg. 12

Enlightenment and inspiration: _____

_____

_____
_____

Morning Nourishment

Gen.   The name of the first [branch] is Pishon; it is the
2:11-12   one that goes around the whole land of Havilah,
where there is gold. And the gold of that land is
good; bdellium and onyx stone are there.
Rev.   And the building work of its wall was jasper; and
21:18   the city was pure gold, like clear glass.
21   And the twelve gates were twelve pearls; each one
of the gates was, respectively, of one pearl...

The flow of the river issued in three precious materials: gold, bdellium, and onyx. These materials typify the Triune God as the basic elements of the structure of God's eternal building. Gold typifies God the Father with His divine nature, which man may partake of through God's calling (2 Pet. 1:3-4), as the base of God's eternal building; bdellium, a pearl-like material produced from the resin of a tree, typifies the produce of God the Son in His redeeming and life-releasing death (John 19:34) and His life-dispensing resurrection (John 12:24; 1 Pet. 1:3), as the entry into God's eternal building (cf. Rev. 21:21 and footnote 1, par. 1); and onyx, a precious stone, typifies the produce of God the Spirit with His transforming work (2 Cor. 3:18) for the building up of God's eternal building. The New Jerusalem is constructed of these three categories of materials—gold, pearl, and precious stones (Rev. 21:11, 18-21). See footnote 21[1], paragraph 2, in Revelation 21.

The flowing of the divine life in man brings the divine nature into man (2 Pet. 1:4), regenerates man (1 Pet. 1:3), and transforms man into the glorious image of Christ (2 Cor. 3:18). Thus, man, who was created of dust (Gen. 2:7), becomes transformed precious materials for God's building, which will consummate in the New Jerusalem. (Gen. 2:12, footnote 1)

Today's Reading

Gold, silver, and precious stones signify the various experiences of Christ in the virtues and attributes of the Triune God. It is with these that the apostles and all spiritual believers build the church on the unique foundation of Christ. Gold may signify the divine nature of the Father with all its attributes, silver may signify the redeeming Christ with all the virtues and attributes of His person and work, and precious stones may signify the transforming work of the Spirit with all its attributes. All these precious materials are the products of our participation in and enjoyment of Christ in our spirit through the Holy Spirit. Only these are good for God's building.

As God's cultivated land with planting, watering, and growing, the church should produce plants; but the proper materials for the building of the church are gold, silver, and precious stones, all of which are minerals. Hence, the thought of transformation is implied here. We need not only to grow in life but also to be transformed in life. (1 Cor. 3:12, footnote 2)

The church is a farm to grow Christ. Every item of the produce grown on the farm is Christ. The farm produce includes many different aspects of Christ. Christ is the milk, the vegetables, and the meat. The church grows Christ, and all the saints eat Christ. Eventually, through digestion, assimilation, and metabolism, Christ becomes us, and we become Him. Then we are the proper materials for the building.

I hope that all the saints in the Lord's recovery will see that we are God's farm to grow Christ and also God's building, His dwelling place. We need the genuine building. To have this building we must grow by having ourselves reduced and by having Christ increased within us. The result of this genuine growth and building is that we do not have preferences for any person, matter, or thing. It also means that we do not have any choice of place. We are happy simply to be members in the Lord's Body, growing in Christ. If this is our condition, then wherever we may be, we shall coordinate with all the saints, no matter whether they are kind or coarse. The real building is to have ourselves reduced and to have Christ increased until we arrive at the measure of the stature of the fullness of Christ. (*Life-study of 1 Corinthians,* pp. 273, 269)

Further Reading: Life-study of 1 Corinthians, msgs. 30-31

Enlightenment and inspiration: _____

_____

_____

_____

Morning Nourishment

Gen. And Jehovah God built the rib, which He had
2:22 taken from the man, into a woman and brought
her to the man.
Eph. Husbands, love your wives even as Christ also
5:25-27 loved the church and gave Himself up for her that
He might sanctify her, cleansing *her* by the washing of the water in the word, that He might present
the church to Himself glorious...

In order to produce a complement for Himself, God first became a man (John 1:14), as typified by God's creation of Adam (Rom. 5:14)....Adam's deep sleep for the producing of Eve as his wife typifies Christ's death on the cross for the producing of the church as His counterpart (Eph. 5:25-27). Through Christ's death the divine life within Him was released, and through His resurrection His released divine life was imparted into His believers for the constituting of the church (see footnote 34[1] in John 19). Through such a process God in Christ has been wrought into man with His life and nature so that man can be the same as God in life and nature in order to match Him as His counterpart. (Gen. 2:21, footnote 1)

The rib taken from Adam's opened side typifies the unbreakable, indestructible eternal life of Christ (Heb. 7:16), which flowed out of His pierced side (John 19:34) to impart life to His believers for the producing and building up of the church as His complement. (Gen. 2:21, footnote 2)

Today's Reading

[Genesis 2:22] does not say that Eve was created but that she was built. The building of Eve with the rib taken from Adam's side typifies the building of the church with the resurrection life released from Christ through His death on the cross and imparted into His believers in His resurrection (John 12:24; 1 Pet. 1:3). The church as the real Eve is the totality of Christ in all His believers. Only that which comes out of Christ with His resurrection life can be His complement and counterpart, the Body of Christ (1 Cor. 12:12; Eph. 5:28-30). (Gen. 2:22, footnote 1)

As Eve was taken out of Adam and brought back to Adam to be one flesh with him (Gen. 2:24), so the church produced out of Christ will go back to Christ (Eph. 5:27; Rev. 19:7) to be one spirit with Him (1 Cor. 6:17). (Gen. 2:22, footnote 3)

Firstly, God became a man. Then this man with the divine life and nature was multiplied through death and resurrection into many believers who become the many members to compose the real Eve to match Him and to complement Him. It is through this process that God in Christ has been wrought into man with His life and nature that man in life and nature can be the same as He is in order to match Him as His complement.

When Adam awoke from his sleep, he immediately discovered that Eve, who was builded with his rib, was present. Likewise, when Christ was resurrected from the dead (1 Cor. 15:20), the church was brought forth with His divine life. Through His death the divine life within Him was released and through His resurrection this released, divine life was imparted into us who believe in Him. So, the Bible says that through His resurrection we were regenerated (1 Pet. 1:3). He was the grain of wheat that fell into the ground and died and produced many grains (John 12:24). We are the many grains who have been regenerated with His resurrection life. As regenerated ones who have Him as life and who live by Him, we compose His church, the real Eve in resurrection.

When Adam saw Eve he said, "This time this is bone of my bones and flesh of my flesh" (Gen. 2:23). When Christ saw the church He might have said, "I have seen the cattle, lions, turtles, fishes, and birds, but none of them could match Me. This time it is bone of My bones and flesh of My flesh, for the church is produced by My death and resurrection. The church comes out of Me. The church and I can be one." *(Life-study of Genesis,* pp. 219-221)

Further Reading: Life-study of Genesis, msg. 17; *The Central Thought of God,* chs. 4-5; *The Central Line of the Divine Revelation,* msg. 7*

Enlightenment and inspiration: _____

_____

_____

_____

Hymns, **#972**

1   Lo, the central thought of God
Is that He be one with man;
He to man is everything
That He might fulfill His plan.

2   Earthen vessel man was made —
Body, soul, and spirit too,
God as life that he may take
And with Him have oneness true.

3   By the flow of life divine,
Man becomes a precious stone
Fit for building God's abode,
That His glory might be known.

4   'Tis the city God hath built,
'Tis the dwelling God requires,
'Tis the new Jerusalem
Which fulfills His heart's desires.

5   'Tis the building of the saints,
'Tis the blend of God and man,
Purposed by the Father's will
Long before the world began.

6   In its center, as its pow'r,
Is the throne of Christ and God,
Whence doth flow the stream of life
As the Spirit's living flood.

7   Christ, the tree of life, is there
In the flowing of the stream,
Yielding fruit of life divine
As the food of life supreme.

8   God in Christ, the glorious light,
Thru the city brightly shines,
Scattering all the deathly night
With its light of life divine.

9   God in man and man in God
Mutual dwelling thus possess;
God the content is to man,
And the man doth God express.

Composition for prophecy with main point and sub-points: _____

_____
_____
_____
_____
_____
_____
_____
_____
_____
_____
_____
_____
_____
_____
_____
_____
_____
_____
_____
_____
_____
_____
_____
_____
_____
_____
_____
_____
_____
_____
_____
_____
_____
_____
_____

Creation in Christ
for the Fulfillment of God's Purpose

Scripture Reading: Gen. 1:1; Rev. 4:11; John 1:3; Heb. 1:2; 11:3; Rev. 3:14; Col. 1:15-17

Day 1   I. **"In the beginning God created the heavens and the earth" (Gen. 1:1):**
   A. *Beginning* here refers to the beginning of time (cf. John 1:1):
      1. Time began at the creation of the universe and continues until the final judgment at the great white throne (Rev. 20:11-15).
      2. Time is for the accomplishing of God's eternal purpose, which God made in eternity past for eternity future (Eph. 3:11).
   B. The Hebrew word for *God* in Genesis 1:1 is *Elohim,* meaning "the Mighty One"; the Hebrew name here is plural, but the verb *created* is singular; this is a seed of the Trinity:
      1. God is one, but He is also three—the Father, the Son, and the Spirit (Isa. 45:5; 1 Cor. 8:4; 1 Tim. 2:5; Matt. 28:19).
      2. God is the Triune God; it was the Triune God who created.
   C. God is the unique Creator; only God can create (Mark 13:19; Eph. 3:9; Rev. 4:11):
      1. The word *created* in Genesis 1:1 means to bring something into existence out of nothing.
      2. God is the One "who made the world and all things in it" (Acts 17:24); He is "the living God, who made heaven and earth and the sea and all things in them" (14:15).

Day 2   D. The motive of God's creation was to fulfill God's desire and to satisfy His good pleasure (Eph. 1:5, 9).
   E. The purpose of God's creation is to glorify the Son of God and to manifest God Himself, especially in man through His Son, who is the

embodiment of God and the image, the expression, of God (Col. 1:15-19; 2:9; Psa. 19:1-2; Rom. 1:20; 1 Tim. 3:16).

II. **"You have created all things, and because of Your will they were, and were created" (Rev. 4:11):**

A. The basis of God's work in creation was God's will and plan (Eph. 1:9-10):

1. God has a will, and according to this will, He conceived His plan (3:11).

2. According to His will and plan, He created all things (v. 9).

B. God's will is God's wish; God's will is what He wants to do (1:9):

1. God's good pleasure is of God's will; His good pleasure is embodied in His will, so His will comes first (v. 5).

2. God's will is His determination for the carrying out of His purpose (v. 11; 1 Cor. 1:1).

Day 3   C. God is a God of purpose, having a will of His own pleasure, and He created all things for His will so that He might accomplish and fulfill His purpose (Rev. 4:11; Eph. 3:9-11; Col. 1:9):

1. God's will is His heart's desire, His mingling with man, and the fulfillment of His eternal plan (Eph. 1:5, 9, 11; 5:17).

2. The will of God is to obtain a Body for Christ to be His fullness, His expression (Rom. 12:2, 5; Eph. 1:5, 9, 11, 22-23).

3. God's creation of the heavens and of the earth began the fulfillment of His eternal plan to carry out His intention to have a full expression in man in the universe (Gen. 1:1; Eph. 3:11, 21).

D. We need to be filled with the full knowledge of God's will (Col. 1:9):

1. God's will in Colossians 1:9 is His will regarding His eternal purpose, regarding His economy concerning Christ (Eph. 1:5, 9, 11).

      2. To have the full knowledge of God's will is to have the revelation of God's plan so that we may know what God plans to do in the universe (Rev. 4:11).

Day 4   **III. "All things came into being through Him [the Word], and apart from Him not one thing came into being which has come into being" (John 1:3):**

    A. Although creation was God's work, the means of His creation were the Son of God and the Word of God (Col. 1:15-16; Heb. 1:2; 11:3; John 1:3; Psa. 33:6, 9).

    B. Since God is the Creator of all things and since Christ is God, Christ is the Creator of all things and also the means through which all things came into being (Heb. 1:10; Psa. 102:25).

    C. In John 1:3 we see that all things came into being through Christ as the Word:

      1. For all things to come into being through Him and for nothing to come into being apart from Him means that apart from Him nothing has existence (v. 3).

      2. Creation is calling things not being as being through the Word; the Word is both the means and the sphere (Rom. 4:17; Heb. 11:3; John 1:3).

      3. Through Christ as the Word, the means, all things came into being; therefore, Christ is both the Creator and the means by which and through which all things were created (Heb. 1:10; John 1:3).

Day 5   D. Christ upholds "all things by the word of His power" (Heb. 1:3):

      1. After creating all things, Christ became the Upholder of all things; He is not only the Creator and the means of creation but also the Upholder.

      2. He created the universe, and now He upholds it by the word of His power.

E. Christ is "the beginning of the creation of God"; this refers to the Lord as the origin or source of God's creation, implying that He is the unchanging and ever-existing source of God's work (Rev. 3:14).

IV. **"In Him all things were created, in the heavens and on the earth...; all things have been created through Him and unto Him...And all things cohere in Him" (Col. 1:16-17):**

A. *In Him* means in the power of Christ's person (v. 16):

1. All things were created in the power of what Christ is.

2. All creation bears the characteristics of Christ's intrinsic power.

B. *Through Him* indicates that Christ is the active instrument through which the creation of all things was accomplished in sequence (v. 16).

C. *Unto Him* indicates that Christ is the end of all creation; all things were created unto Him for His possession (v. 16).

Day 6   D. *In, through,* and *unto* indicate that Christ is related to creation in a subjective way (v. 16):

1. He did not create the universe merely in an objective way, as an objective Creator.

2. Christ did not stand apart and call everything into being; on the contrary, the process of creation took place in the power of His person, the unique power in the universe.

3. He was not merely an objective Creator but also the subjective instrument through which creation was processed.

4. Creation took place in the power of Christ's person, through Him as the active instrument, and unto Him as the goal.

E. *All things cohere in Him* means that all things cohere, subsist together, in Christ as the holding center, just as the spokes of a wheel are held together by the hub at their center (v. 17).

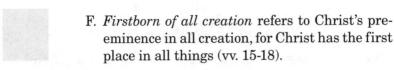

F. *Firstborn of all creation* refers to Christ's pre-eminence in all creation, for Christ has the first place in all things (vv. 15-18).

Morning Nourishment

Gen. **In the beginning God created the heavens and the**
1:1 **earth.**

Eph. **And to enlighten all** *that they may see* **what the econ-**
3:9 **omy of the mystery is, which throughout the ages**
has been hidden in God, who created all things.

The Bible begins with the words, "In the beginning." However, what Genesis 1:1 says is different from John 1:1....Although two books, Genesis and John, start with the same phrase, the meaning of each is absolutely different. The phrase *in the beginning* in Genesis denotes the beginning of time, for it refers to God's creation. Therefore Genesis 1:1 refers to the beginning of time in which God created all things. The meaning of this phrase in John 1:1 is different, for it refers to eternity in the past without a beginning. The beginning in Genesis 1 starts from the time of creation, but the beginning in John 1 is before the time of creation. In other words, the beginning in Genesis 1 is the beginning of time, and the beginning in John is the beginning before time existed; it refers to eternity past without a beginning. (*Life-study of John,* pp. 17-18)

Today's Reading

Time began at the creation of the universe and continues until the final judgment at the great white throne (Rev. 20:11-15). Time is for the accomplishing of God's eternal purpose, which God made in eternity past (Eph. 3:11) for eternity future. (Gen. 1:1, footnote 2)

[*God* in Genesis 1:1 is the Hebrew word] *Elohim,* meaning *the Mighty One.* The Hebrew name here is plural, but the verb *created* is singular. Furthermore, in verse 26 the plural pronouns *Us* and *Our* are used in reference to God, whereas in verse 27 the pronouns *He* and *His* are used. These are seeds of the Trinity. God is one (Isa. 45:5; 1 Cor. 8:4; 1 Tim. 2:5), but He is also three—the Father, the Son, and the Spirit (Matt. 28:19). He is the Triune God. It was the Triune God who created. (Gen. 1:1, footnote 3)

Only God can create. To create means to bring something into existence out of nothing. God is the unique Creator. (*The Conclusion of the New Testament,* p. 146)

In Acts 17:24 Paul speaks of the God who made the world and all things in it. This word was directed mainly against the Epicureans, who, as atheists, did not believe in God. They believed neither in the Creator nor in the divine provision. Therefore, continuing to speak against the Epicureans, Paul went on to say that God is the Lord of heaven and earth. This One was absolutely ignored by the Epicureans. Furthermore, Paul pointed out that God Himself gives to all life and breath and all things. These are the divine provisions. God provides all things so that man may live. The Epicureans did not believe in the Creator, the Lord of heaven and earth who provides all the necessities of life for human beings.

Paul's preaching in Acts 17 is very good. When he was reasoning with the Jews in the synagogues, he used the Scriptures. But when he was preaching to the philosophical Epicureans, he referred to the creation.

What Paul did in 17:2 and 17:24 and 25 is similar to what he did in chapters 13 and 14. In chapter 13 he used the Jewish Scriptures as the basis for preaching the resurrected Christ. But in chapter 14 his preaching to the heathen was based on God's creation. However, there is a difference in Paul's use of the creation in his preaching in chapters 14 and 17; his utterance in these chapters is somewhat different. In chapter 14 he told the heathen that the "living God, who made heaven and earth and the sea and all things in them...did not leave Himself without witness, in that He did good by giving you rain from heaven and fruitful seasons, filling your hearts with food and gladness" (14:15, 17). There his word was not very philosophical. By contrast, Paul's word to counter the false teachings of the Epicureans in chapter 17 is quite philosophical. Here Paul declares that there is a Creator, the Lord of heaven and earth, and that He provides life, breath, and everything necessary for man's living on earth. (*Life-study of Acts,* pp. 404-405)

Further Reading: Life-study of John, msg. 2; *Life-study of Acts,* msg. 47

Enlightenment and inspiration: _____

_____

_____

_____

Morning Nourishment

**Eph. Making known to us the mystery of His will ac-
1:9 cording to His good pleasure, which He purposed
in Himself.**

**Rev. You are worthy, our Lord and God, to receive the
4:11 glory and the honor and the power, for You have
created all things, and because of Your will they
were, and were created.**

Created [in Genesis 1:1], denoting to bring something into existence out of nothing, differs from *made* in 2:4 and *formed* in 2:7, the latter two denoting to take something that already exists and use it to produce something else.

The motive of God's creation was to fulfill God's desire and to satisfy His good pleasure (Eph. 1:5, 9). The purpose of God's creation is to glorify the Son of God (Col. 1:15-19) and to manifest God Himself (Psa. 19:1-2; Rom. 1:20...), especially in man (1 Tim. 3:16) through His Son, Christ, who is the embodiment of God and the image, the expression, of God (Col. 2:9; 1:15). The basis of God's creation is God's will and plan (Eph. 1:10...). The means of God's creation were the Son of God (Col. 1:15-16; Heb. 1:2b) and the Word of God (Heb. 11:3; John 1:1-3), both of whom are Christ (John 1:1, 18; Rev. 19:13). (Gen. 1:1, footnote 4)

Today's Reading

God's creation...reveals His desire in the universe and manifests His purpose in eternity. Anything we make expresses our desire. Although we may not say much, the thing we make manifests our purpose. When God created the heavens, the earth with so many items, and eventually man in His own image and with authority over all created things, He surely had a purpose. By His creation we can see that God had a desire and a purpose.

According to Ephesians 1:5 and 9, the motive of God's original creation was His desire and pleasure. God carried out the original creation to fulfill His desire and to satisfy His pleasure. He desired and liked to create; so He did it to please Himself.

The basis of creation is God's will and plan (Eph. 1:10). Reve-

lation 4:11 tells us clearly that all things were created according
to God's will. God has a will, and according to that will He conceived His plan. According to that will and plan He created all
things. (*Life-study of Genesis,* pp. 9-10)

We have seen that the central line of the divine revelation
starts from God. Then the divine revelation shows us the divine
economy and the divine dispensing. God Himself, God's economy, and God's dispensing can be seen throughout the entire
Bible. These three items are the central line of the divine revelation. The divine revelation reveals to us three main entities: God
Himself, God's economy, and God's dispensing.

The divine economy is an issue of God's will, purpose, good
pleasure, and counsel....God's will is God's wish, God's desire.
God's will is what He wishes to do and wants to do. God's good
pleasure is of God's will. Ephesians 1:5 speaks of "the good pleasure of His will." His good pleasure is embodied in His will, so
His will comes first. God's will was hidden in God as a mystery,
so Ephesians 1:9 speaks of "the mystery of His will." In eternity
God planned a will. This will was hidden in Him; hence, it was a
mystery. God's will as a mystery hidden in God issues in God's
economy, dispensation (3:9). From God's will issues God's economy through His purpose, good pleasure, and counsel. (*The Central Line of the Divine Revelation,* pp. 32-33)

In 1 Corinthians 1:1 Paul says that he was an apostle
through the will of God. The will of God is His determination for
the carrying out of His purpose. Through this will Paul was called
to be an apostle of Christ....The will of God here is related to God's
administration, to God's government. Paul was called according
to God's will and under God's administration to carry out God's
New Testament economy. This is a matter of great significance.
Paul was appointed and called according to God's will to carry
out His administration. (*Life-study of 1 Corinthians,* p. 7)

Further Reading: Life-study of Genesis, msg. 1; *The Central Line
of the Divine Revelation,* msg. 3

Enlightenment and inspiration: _____

_____

_____

_____

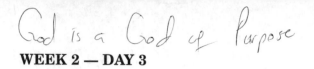
God is a God of Purpose

Morning Nourishment

Col. ...That you may be filled with the full knowledge of
1:9 His will in all spiritual wisdom and understanding.
Eph. Predestinating us unto sonship through Jesus Christ
1:5 to Himself, according to the good pleasure of His will.
11 In whom also we were designated as an inheritance, having been predestinated according to the
purpose of the One who works all things according
to the counsel of His will.

God is a God of purpose, having a will of His own pleasure. He
created all things for His will that He might accomplish and fulfill His purpose. [The book of Revelation], which unveils God's
universal administration, shows us the purpose of God. Hence,
in the twenty-four elders' praise to God concerning His creation
[in 4:11], His creation is related to His will. (Rev. 4:11, footnote 2)

Today's Reading

God's will is not only His heart desire and His mingling with
man but also the fulfillment of His plan....Many people ask, "Is
it God's will that I go to a certain place today? Is it His will that I
seek a doctor for my sickness? Is it His will that I seek this occu-
pation?" We miserable beings can never forget ourselves when
we mention the will of God! Nor can we be separated from the
trivial matters of life! We always view the will of God from an
earthly standpoint, from our present situation, and from ourselves. Actually, none of these trivial matters of life can come up
to the will of God! How great and how high is the will of God!

The book of Ephesians reveals to us God's heart desire and
God's plan. God's plan in Christ originated from His heart
desire. God in eternity had a plan, which He purposed to fulfill.
This plan is the will of God. Therefore, the will of God is for the
fulfillment of His plan. All the works of God in this universe are
according to His will and for the fulfillment of His plan. (*The
Experience of Life,* p. 161)

The Body is not mentioned in the thirty-nine books of the
Old Testament. The first mentioning of the Body in the New

Testament is in Romans 12:5. According to Romans 12, we must present our physical bodies (v. 1) for the mystical Body of Christ (v. 5). When we present our bodies and are renewed in our mind, we see, discern, and prove by testing that the will of God is to obtain a Body for Christ to be His fullness and expression (v. 2). (*The Central Line of the Divine Revelation,* p. 268)

As the Creator of the heavens and the earth, Christ is the origination and the source of all the created things. This proves that He is the very God who is over all and is blessed forever (Rom. 9:5b). His creation of the heavens and of the earth began the fulfillment of God's eternal plan to carry out God's intention to have a full expression in man in the universe. (*The Conclusion of the New Testament,* p. 675)

God's will [in Colossians 1:9] refers to the will of His eternal purpose, of His economy concerning Christ (Eph. 1:5, 9, 11), not His will in minor things....Years ago, when young saints asked about things such as marriage or employment, I referred them to this verse in Colossians. I told them that they should seek spiritual knowledge in order to know God's will. But the will of God here is not focused on things such as marriage, jobs, or housing; it is concerned with the all-inclusive Christ as our portion. The will of God for us is that we know the all-inclusive Christ, experience Him, and live Him as our life. To know Christ in this way is to have the full knowledge of God's will. (*Life-study of Colossians,* p. 19)

[Colossians 1:9 speaks] of being filled with "the full knowledge of His will." To be filled with the full knowledge of God's will simply means to have the revelation of God's plan, so that through this revelation we know what God plans to do in this universe. As believers we have to know God's universal plan. What did God plan in eternity past to do in time throughout all the generations? We need such a revelation so that we can have the full knowledge of God's eternal plan. (*The Mystery of God and the Mystery of Christ,* p. 29)

Further Reading: The Experience of Life, ch. 8; *Life-study of Colossians,* msg. 3

Enlightenment and inspiration: _____

_____

_____

_____

Morning Nourishment

John **All things came into being through Him, and apart**
1:3 **from Him not one thing came into being which has**
come into being.
Heb. **And, "You in the beginning, Lord, laid the founda-**
1:10 **tion of the earth, and the heavens are the works of**
Your hands."

Although creation was God's work, the means of His creation
were the Son of God (Col. 1:15-16; Heb. 1:2b) and the Word of God
(Heb. 11:3; John 1:1-3). The New Testament clearly tells us that
God created the universe through Christ as the Son of God and
the Word of God. Speaking of Christ as the means of creation,
Colossians 1:16 says, "Because in Him all things were created, in the
heavens and on the earth, the visible and the invisible, whether
thrones or lordships or rulers or authorities; all things have been
created through Him and unto Him." Regarding Christ as the
Word, John 1:3 says, "All things came into being through Him,
and apart from Him not one thing came into being which has
come into being." (*The Conclusion of the New Testament,* p. 146)

Today's Reading

Christ is the Creator. Since God is the Creator of all things and
since Christ is God, He surely is also the Creator of all things.
This is clearly revealed in Hebrews 1:10....This verse, a quota-
tion from Psalm 102:25, is applied to Christ the Son and indicates that, as God, Christ created heaven and earth. Therefore,
Christ is the Creator of the universe. (*The Conclusion of the New
Testament,* p. 269)

The creation came into being through the Word. I like the
way the Recovery Version of John renders 1:3. "All things came into
being through Him, and apart from Him not one thing came
into being which has come into being." What does it mean that
all things came into being through Him and that apart from
Him nothing has come into being? It simply means that apart
from Him nothing has existence. One day, through the Word, so
many things came into being. We may say that, in a sense, God

Genesis 1:26-28

God said, Let Us make man in Our image,
g to Our likeness; and let them have
n over the fish of the sea and over the birds
n and over the cattle and over all the earth
r every creeping thing that creeps upon the

God created man in His own image; in the
God He created him; male and female He
nem.

God blessed them; and God said to them, Be
nd multiply, and fill the earth and subdue it,
dominion over the fish of the sea and over
of heaven and over every living thing that
on the earth.

s : *Genesis 1:26*[1, 2, 3, 4, 5, 6], *28*[1]

Life Study Messages
Genesis LS # 6 – Whole message

5/19	Genesis 1:26

give heed to myths and unending
es, which produce questionings rather than
iomy, which is in faith.

does not love has not known God, because
e.

is the message which we have heard from
nnounce to you, that God is light and in
darkness at all.

four living creatures, each one of them
wings apiece, are full of eyes around and
they have no rest day and night, saying,
holy, Lord God the Almighty, who was
nd who is coming.

ys Judah will be saved, And Israel will
ely; And this is His name by which He
d, Jehovah our righteousness.

ho is joined to the Lord is one spirit.

Genesis 1:26[1, 2, 3]

eading: *Life Study of Genesis, #6, pp. 62*
12) *The Conference of the Godhead*

Making the Believers God-Men [paragraphs 2-3]).
Crystallization Study of Genesis HWMR – Week 4—
Day 3

Thursday 5/22	Gen. 1:26-28

John 1:1, 14
1 In the beginning was the Word, and the Word was
with God, and the Word was God.

14 And the Word became flesh and tabernacled
among us (and we beheld His glory, glory as of the
only Begotten from the Father), full of grace and
reality.

Luke 1:31-32
31 And behold, you will conceive in *your* womb and
bear a son, and you shall call His name Jesus.
32 He will be great and will be called Son of the
Most High; and the Lord God will give to Him the
throne of David His father,

Luke 19:9-10
9 And Jesus said to him, Today salvation has come to
this house, because he also is a son of Abraham.
10 For the Son of Man has come to seek and to save
that which is lost.

1 Cor. 15:45b
45b ....the last Adam *became* a life-giving Spirit.

Rom. 5:10
10 For if we, being enemies, were reconciled to God
through the death of His Son, much more we will be
saved in His life, having been reconciled,

Rom. 12:2
2 And do not be fashioned according to this age, but
be transformed by the renewing of the mind that you
may prove what the will of God is, that which is good
and well pleasing and perfect.

Footnotes: Genesis 1:26[4.]
Suggested Reading: Genesis 1:26[4]; *The Central*
Thought of God, p. 17 (Section: The Main Items of
Creation in Genesis 1 [paragraphs 11-12a]); Truth
Lessons—Level Three, Vol. 1, pp. 19-21(Section: I.
Adam Typifying Christ [paragraph 1a]; Sections A.
B. C. D. E.); Life Study of Luke, #57, pp. 491-492
(Sections: Gods Intention in the Creation of Man
[paragraph 2]; The Second Man [paragraph 1];
Living a Human Life Filled with the Divine Life); Life
Study of 1& 2 Chronicles, #4, pp. 27-28 (Section:
Revolutionized By Realizing that We are God-Men
[paragraph 2]); Life Study of Luke, #58-59, pp. 505,
498-499, 507 (Sections: Uplifting the Human Virtues
to the Highest Standard; To Fill the Empty Human

Virtues [sentence 1]; To Strengthen and Enrich the Human Virtues [paragraph 2]; Producing the Highest Stand of Morality For the Saving Power of the Man-Savior's Dynamic Salvation [paragraph 7]; Crystallization Study of Genesis HWMR – Week 4— Days 4-5

Friday 5/23

Rev. 4:3
3 And He who was sitting was like a jasper stone and a sardius in appearance, and *there was* a rainbow around the throne like an emerald in appearance.

Rev. 21:11, 18
11 Having the glory of God. Her light was like a most precious stone, like a jasper stone, as clear as crystal.

18 And the building work of its wall was jasper; and the city was pure gold, like clear glass.

Phil. 2:6-8
6 Who, existing in the form of God, did not consider being equal with God a treasure to be grasped,
7 But emptied Himself, taking the form of a slave, becoming in the likeness of men;
8 And being found in fashion as a man, He humbled Himself, becoming obedient even unto death, and *that* the death of a cross.

1 Pet, 1:3
3 Blessed be the God and Father of our Lord Jesus Christ, who according to His great mercy has regenerated us unto a living hope through the resurrection of Jesus Christ from the dead,

1 John 5:11-12
11 And this is the testimony, that God gave to us eternal life and this life is in His Son.
12 He who has the Son has the life; he who does not have the Son of God does not have the life.

Suggested Reading: Truth Lessons—Level Three, Vol. 3, pp. 33 (Section: I. D. Into the Image of Christ [paragraphs 1-3]); The Conclusion of the New Testament, p. 3081-3082 (Section: 13. The Firstborn of God [paragraph 4]. a. Having Been Predestinated to Be Conformed to His Image); The Basic Revelation in the Holy Scriptures, pp. 145 (Section: A Corporate Expression of God) Crystallization Study of Genesis HWMR – Week 4— Day 6

Saturday 5/24   Genesis 1:26-28

Eph. 3:17a; 2 Cor. 3:16-18; John 12:24-25; Rom. 8:28-29; Heb. 2:12; John 1:1, 14; Rev. 4:3;

21:11; Phil. 2:6-8; 1 John 5:11-

Lord's Day 5/25   Psalm 139:

Psalm 139:1-16 (1-8, 13-16)
1 O Jehovah, You have searched m
2 You know when I sit down and understand my thoughts from afar
3 You thoroughly search my patl And You are acquainted with all r
4 For a word is not yet on my tor O Jehovah, know it completely.
5 You have closed in on me b have laid Your hand on me.
6 O knowledge too wonderful 1 cannot attain to it.
7 Where shall I go, away from shall I flee from Your presence?
8 If I ascend into heaven, You bed in Sheol, there You are.
9 If I take the wings of the daw of the sea,
10 There also Your hand will hand will take hold of me.
11 And if I say, Surely darknes light around me will be night;
12 Even the darkness is not shines like day; The darkness i
13 For it was You who form wove me together in my moth
14 I will praise You, for wonderfully made; Your wor soul knows it well.
15 My frame was not hidde made in secret, Skillfully fas earth.
16 Your eyes saw my unforr book all of them were w ordained for me, When not o

* For expanded version of to www.churchinnyc.org

The Church in
                Qu
87-60 Chevy Chase St.
Jamaica Estates, NY 11432
(718) 454-1826

Manhattan
446 W. 34th St.
New York, NY
(212) 268-5795

w w w . c h u

Mor

26 And accordi domini of hea and ov earth.
27 And image c created
28 And fruitful and hav the bird moves u

Footnot

Monday

1 Tim. 1:
4 Nor t genealog God's ec

1 John 4:
8 He who God is lo

1 John 1:
5 And thi Him and Him is no

Rev. 4:8
8 And the having six within; an Holy, holy and who is

Jer. 23:6
6 In His d dwell secu will be call

1 Cor. 6:17
17 But he v

Footnotes:
Suggested .
(Sections:

did not make anything, for there was no need for Him to do anything. He simply said, "Being," and everything had being. According to our human concept, creation requires a certain amount of labor. However, in God's creation there was no labor, only speaking....An atheist would say that this is nonsense, because he does not believe in God. But we believe in Him. We not only believe in God, but also in the all-inclusive Christ. Through Him as the Word all things came into being.

Creation is calling things not being as being through the Word. The Word is both the means and the sphere. As long as you have the Word, you have the means and the sphere. Thus, you can say, "Because I have the Word as the means and the sphere, things not being can come into being." Learn to say, "Not being as being through the Word." No longer am I apart from the Word. I am in the Word and with the Word. Hence, through the Word things not being come into being. (*Life-study of John*, pp. 21-23)

We may not differentiate Christ as the Creator from Christ as the means of creation. Even we may interpret John 1:3 as meaning that the Word is the Creator of all things. However, this verse does not say that the Word was the Creator; instead, this verse says that through the Word all things came into being, indicating that the Word was the means through which the Creator created all things. Christ is both the Creator and the means by which all things were created.

Although as God Christ is the Creator, John 1:3 reveals that as the Word He was the means of creation. According to this verse, all things came into existence through Christ. The King James Version of John 1:3 says, "All things were made by him." However, this is not an accurate translation. The Greek preposition should be rendered "through" and not "by." Hence, this verse does not say that all things were created by Christ but that all things came into existence through Christ. This indicates that Christ is the means of creation. (*The Conclusion of the New Testament*, p. 270)

Further Reading: The Conclusion of the New Testament, msgs. 14, 25

Enlightenment and inspiration: _____

_____

_____

_____

Morning Nourishment

Col. **Because in Him all things were created, in the**
1:16-17 **heavens and on the earth, the visible and the invis-**
ible, whether thrones or lordships or rulers or
authorities; all things have been created through
Him and unto Him. And He is before all things, and
all things cohere in Him.

Hebrews 1:3 tells us that Christ upholds "all things by the word
of His power." After creating all things, Christ became the Upholder of all things. The earth is suspended in space. There is
nothing visible supporting it. After Christ created the earth, He
began to uphold it, and He upholds it now by the word of His power.
If you ask scientists what upholds the earth, they will say
only that something upholds it. The earth is one of many planets. Astronomers tell us that all the planets move according to
their own track. If they were to move out of orbit, there would be
a global accident. Who upholds all the planets and the whole
universe? Christ upholds all things, and He upholds them very
easily. There is no need for Him to do anything—He simply
speaks. He upholds all things by the word of His power. (*The
Conclusion of the New Testament,* p. 278)

Today's Reading

The book of Hebrews emphasizes the word of God. Hebrews
11:3 says that the universe was framed by the word of God. Now
we see in 1:3 that the universe is upheld by the word of Christ's
power. The divine word is powerful. Christ is not only the Creator
and the means of creation; He is also the Upholder. He created
the universe, and now He upholds the universe by His word.
Speaking of Christ, Colossians 1:17 says, "All things subsist
together in Him" [Darby]. *Subsist together in Him* [or *cohere*]
means to exist together by Christ as the holding center, just as
the spokes of a wheel are held together by the hub at their
center. For creation to subsist in Christ is a further indication
that Christ is subjectively related to creation.
It is important to differentiate between the words *exist, consist,*

and *subsist*....To exist is to be, to consist is to be composed or constituted, and to subsist is to be held together for existence. Imagine a wheel with its rim, spokes, and hub. All the spokes subsist together in the hub. The only way for the spokes to subsist is to be held together at the hub in the center of the wheel. This illustrates Christ's relationship to creation with respect to the fact that all things subsist in Him.

All things came into being in Christ, through Christ, and unto Christ. Nothing should be regarded as separate from Him. All things were made in the intrinsic power of Christ's person, through Him as the active instrument, and unto Him as the consummate goal. Furthermore, all things subsist, [cohere], are held together, in Him as the hub. Because all things were created in Christ, through Christ, and unto Christ and because all things subsist in Christ, God can be expressed in creation through Christ, who is the image of the invisible God. (*The Conclusion of the New Testament,* pp. 278-279)

In Revelation 3:14 the Lord also refers to Himself as "the beginning of the creation of God." This refers to the Lord as the origin or source of God's creation, implying that the Lord is the unchanging and ever-existing source of God's work. This indicates that the degraded recovered church is changing by leaving the Lord as the source. (*Life-study of Revelation,* p. 198)

Colossians 1:16 says, "Because in Him all things were created, in the heavens and on the earth, the visible and the invisible;...all things have been created through Him and unto Him." *In Him* means in the power of Christ's person. All things were created in the power of what Christ is. All creation bears the characteristics of Christ's intrinsic power....*Through Him* indicates that Christ is the active instrument through which the creation of all things was processed. Finally, *unto Him* indicates that Christ is the end of all creation. All things were created for His possession. (*Life-study of Colossians,* p. 69)

Further Reading: The Mystery of God and the Mystery of Christ, chs. 2-3

Enlightenment and inspiration: _____

_____

_____

_____

Morning Nourishment

Col. Who is the image of the invisible God, the First-
1:15 born of all creation.
18 And He is the Head of the Body, the church; He is
the beginning, the Firstborn from the dead, that
He Himself might have the first place in all things.

Christ is related to creation in a subjective way. Christ did
not create the universe merely in an objective way as an objective Creator. He did not, so to speak, stand apart and call everything into being. On the contrary, the process of creation took
place in Him, that is, in the power of His person. Christ is the
unique power in the universe. His very person is this power.
Therefore, creation was processed in Him. This means that He
was not simply an objective Creator, but also the subjective
instrument through which creation was processed. For this
reason, creation bears the characteristics of Christ's intrinsic
power. Instead of saying that Christ created the universe, the
Bible says that all things came into being through Him or were
created in Him. The words *by Him* are objective, whereas the
words *through Him* and *in Him* are subjective. (*Life-study of
Colossians,* p. 81)

Today's Reading

The King James Version of Colossians 1:16 says that all things
have been created for Him. It is better to render the Greek "unto
Him." *For Him* is objective, but *unto Him* is subjective. All things
have been created in Christ, through Christ, and, ultimately, unto
Christ. These expressions indicate that Christ has a subjective
relationship to creation. Creation is not simply for Him; it is also
unto Him. This means that it consummates in Him. The three
prepositions *in, through,* and *unto* were used by Paul to point out
the subjective relationship of Christ to creation. Creation took
place in the power of Christ's person, through Him as the active
instrument, and unto Him as its consummation. Such a relationship is altogether subjective. Because of His subjective relationship to creation, Christ expresses God in creation. Creation

expresses the characteristics of Christ who is the image of the invisible God. (*Life-study of Colossians,* pp. 81-82)

According to the New Testament, the word *subsist* includes, or implies, three things: to exist, to live, and to live together. All things not only exist in Christ but also live, or continue in existence, in Him. Furthermore, all things live together, or exist together, in Him. The entire universe subsists, exists together, in Christ. He is the center in which all things subsist. All things not only exist in Him; all things also live in Him and live together corporately in Him. (*The Conclusion of the New Testament,* p. 279)

In Colossians 1:15 Paul goes on to say that Christ is the First-born of all creation. This means that in creation Christ is the first. Christ as God is the Creator. However, as man, sharing the created blood and flesh (Heb. 2:14), He is part of the creation. "Firstborn of all creation" [Col. 1:15] refers to Christ's preeminence in all creation, since from this verse through verse 18 the apostle stresses the first place of Christ in all things. This verse reveals that Christ is not only the Creator, but also the first among all created things, the first among all creatures.

Some may wonder how Christ could be the Firstborn of all creation since He was born less than two thousand years ago, not at the very beginning of creation. If we would understand this properly, we need to realize that with God there is no time element.

Therefore, according to God's perspective in eternity, Christ was born in eternity past. This is the reason that, according to God's viewpoint, Christ has always been the first of all creatures. God foresaw the day that Christ would be born in a manger in Bethlehem. Because Christ is the first among the creatures, we can say that as the all-inclusive One He is both the Creator and part of creation. (*Life-study of Colossians,* pp. 66-68)

Further Reading: Life-study of Colossians, msgs. 8, 10

Enlightenment and inspiration: _____

_____

_____

_____

Hymns, #189

1 Thou art the Son beloved,
     The image of our God;
  Thou art the saints' dear portion,
     Imparted thru Thy blood.
  Among all God's creation
     Thou art the firstborn One;
  By Thee all was created,
     All for Thyself to own.

2 Thou art before all creatures,
     In Thee all things consist;
  Of all Thou art the center,
     By Thee all things subsist.
  Thou art the sole beginning,
     The Firstborn from the dead;
  And for the Church, Thy Body,
     Thou art the glorious Head.

3 Because it pleased the Father,
     All fulness dwells in Thee,
  That Thou might have the first place
     In all we ever see.
  All things Thou reconciledst
     To God by Thy shed blood,
  To thus present us holy
     And blameless unto God.

4 In Thee God's fulness dwelleth,
     Thou art God's mystery;
  The treasures of all wisdom
     And knowledge are in Thee.
  Thou art the hope of glory,
     In us Thou dost abide;
  In Thee we are perfected
     And God is satisfied.

5 All things are but a shadow
     Which unto us reveal
  Thyself, in whom we're rooted,
     The only One that's real.
  Enjoying all Thy riches,
     Thy fulness we will be;
  We'll hold Thee, as Thy Body,
     And grow with God in Thee.

6   With Thee in God we're hidden,
        Thou art in us our life;
    Thy peace in us presiding,
        We rest from all our strife.
    In the new man, Thy Body,
        Thou art the all in all;
    Our all-inclusive Savior,
        Thyself we'll ever call.

Composition for prophecy with main point and sub-points: _____

_____

_____

_____

_____

_____

_____

_____

_____

_____

_____

_____

_____

_____

_____

_____

_____

_____

_____

_____

_____

_____

_____

_____

_____

_____

_____

_____

_____

The Experience of Christ as Life
Portrayed in Genesis 1

Scripture Reading: Gen. 1:1-31

Day 1 I. **The Spirit, the word, and the light were the instruments used by God to generate life on the first day of His restoration and further creation for the fulfillment of His purpose; the Spirit, the word, and the light are all of life (Gen. 1:1-5; Rom. 8:2; Phil. 2:16; John 8:12b):**

A. Christ as the Spirit is the reality of God (Rom. 8:9-10; 2 Cor. 3:17; John 16:13-15):

1. The Spirit of God, as the Spirit of life (Rom. 8:2), came to brood over the waters of death in order to generate life, especially man, for God's purpose (Gen. 1:2; 2:7; 1:26).

2. In spiritual experience the Spirit's coming is the first requirement for generating life (John 6:63a; 16:8-11).

B. Christ as the Word is the speaking of God (1:1; Heb. 1:2):

1. After the Spirit's brooding, the word of God came to bring in the light (Gen. 1:3; 2 Cor. 4:6; cf. Psa. 119:105, 130).

2. In spiritual experience the coming of the word is the second requirement for generating life (John 5:24; 6:63b).

C. Christ as the light is the shining of God (Gen. 1:3-5; John 1:1, 4-5; 8:12a; 9:5); in spiritual experience the coming of the light is the third requirement for generating life (Matt. 4:13-16; John 1:1-13).

D. The separation of the light from the darkness for the purpose of discerning day from night is the fourth requirement for generating life (Gen. 1:4-5; 2 Cor. 6:14b).

Day 2 II. **The separating of the waters by producing an expanse between them on the second day,**

signifying, spiritually, the dividing of the heavenly things from the earthly things through the
work of the cross, is the fifth requirement
for generating life (Gen. 1:6-8; Col. 3:1-3; Heb.
4:12).

III. **The appearing of the dry land is the sixth
requirement for generating life; this took
place on the third day, corresponding to the
day of resurrection (Gen. 1:9-13; 1 Cor. 15:4):**

A. In the Bible the sea represents death, and the
land represents Christ as the generating source
of life; after the land appeared, every kind of
life—the plant life, the animal life, and even the
human life—was produced out of the land (Gen.
1:11-12, 24-27; 2:7); this typifies that the divine
life with all its riches comes out of Christ.

B. On the third day Christ came out of death in resurrection to generate life for the constituting of
the church (John 12:24; 1 Pet. 1:3).

Day 3 C. Dividing the land from the waters signifies separating life from death; from the second day
(Gen. 1:6-7) God began to work to confine and
limit the waters of death that covered the earth
(cf. Jer. 5:22):

1. Eventually, when God's work is completed,
in the new heaven and new earth there will
be no more sea (Rev. 21:1 and footnote 3,
Recovery Version).

2. Furthermore, in the New Jerusalem there
will be no more night (v. 25 and footnote 2).

3. This means that both death and darkness
will be eliminated.

D. The plant life is the lowest form of life, a life without consciousness, corresponding to the earliest
stage of the divine life in a newly regenerated
believer (Gen. 1:11; cf. 1 Cor. 3:6):

1. The countless varieties of the plant life
typify the rich expression of the unsearchable riches of the life of Christ in their

beauty for man's sight (Gen. 2:9), in their fragrance (S. S. 1:12-13), and in their nourishing man and animals (Gen. 1:29-30).

2. The trees (2:9; Exo. 15:23-25; S. S. 2:3; 5:15; Isa. 11:1; John 15:1; Rev. 22:2), the flowers (S. S. 1:14), and the grains as food for man (John 6:9, 13) and as offerings to God (Lev. 2:1-3, 14) are all types of Christ.

Day 4 IV. **The light-bearers appeared on the fourth day as the seventh requirement for generating life to produce the higher forms of life (Gen. 1:14-19):**

A. According to the revelation of the whole Bible, light is for life; light and life always go together (Psa. 36:9; Matt. 4:16; John 1:4; 8:12; 1 John 1:1-7).

B. Life depends on light, and the higher the light, the higher the life:

1. The indefinite light of the first day (Gen. 1:3) was sufficient for generating the lowest forms of life; the more solid and more definite light from the light-bearers—the sun, the moon, and the stars (v. 16; Psa. 136:7-9)—on the fourth day was necessary for producing the higher forms of life, including the human life.

2. This signifies that for our spiritual rebirth, the light of the "first day" is sufficient, but for the growth in the divine life unto maturity, more and stronger light, the light of the "fourth day," is needed.

3. The light-bearers were for signs, seasons, days, and years (Gen. 1:14), which are all shadows of Christ (Col. 2:16-17).

C. The sun (Psa. 136:8) signifies Christ (Mal. 4:2; Luke 1:78-79; Matt. 4:16; Eph. 5:14); the overcoming saints were also likened to the sun by the Lord Jesus (Matt. 13:43).

D. The moon (Psa. 136:9) can be considered a figure of the church, the wife of Christ (cf. Gen. 37:9; S. S. 6:10):

1. The moon has no light of its own but shines in the night and reflects the light of the sun.
2. Likewise, the church shines in the dark night of the church age by reflecting the divine light of Christ (2 Cor. 3:18; cf. Phil. 2:15).

E. The stars first signify Christ and then the overcomers (Num. 24:17; 2 Pet. 1:19; Rev. 22:16; Dan. 12:3):
1. Although Christ is the real sun, He does not appear as the sun during the present age of night; rather, He shines as the bright morning star (Rev. 22:16).
2. The stars also signify the overcoming saints (Dan. 12:3; cf. Rev. 1:20).
3. The light from the stars is needed particularly when the moon wanes; likewise, the shining of the overcoming saints as the heavenly stars is needed particularly in the time of the church's degradation (2:7, 11, 17, 26-28; 3:5, 12, 20-21).

F. The ruling of the fourth-day light-bearers also strengthened the separating of the light from the darkness in Genesis 1:4; both are requirements for the growth in life.

Day 5 V. **The living creatures in the water and in the air were generated on the fifth day (vv. 20-23):**
A. This is the animal life with the lowest consciousness, corresponding to the first step in the believers' growth in life (cf. 1 John 2:13):
1. The animal life in the sea typifies the riches of the life of Christ in the power that overcomes death (signified by the salt water) in His living; just as fish can live in salt water without becoming salty, Christ and His believers, who have the divine life, can live in the satanic world without being "salted" by the world's corruption (cf. John 14:30; 17:15-16).
2. The animal life in the sea also shows the riches of Christ's life in feeding man with His riches (6:9a; 21:9).

B. The bird life is higher than the fish life; fish can live in the death waters, but birds can transcend the death waters:

1. By growing further in the divine life, the believers are able to transcend all the frustrations of the earth (Isa. 40:31).

2. The bird life typifies the riches of the life of Christ as seen in His being the eagle for carrying God's redeemed to His destination (Exo. 19:4; Deut. 32:11-12; Rev. 12:14) and in His being the turtledoves or pigeons for offering to God for the sins of God's people (Lev. 1:14; 5:7).

Day 6 VI. **The living creatures on the earth were generated on the sixth day (Gen. 1:24-31):**

A. The cattle and the animals on the earth are a higher life with a higher consciousness than that of the fish and the birds, a life that can accomplish something on the earth:

1. The animals and the cattle on the land typify the riches of the life of Christ as seen in Christ as the conquering lion (Rev. 5:5) to fight for God's economy, as seen in Christ as the sheep and oxen for offering to God for the fulfillment of God's full redemption (Lev. 1:2-3, 10; 3:1, 6, 12; 4:3; 5:6; John 1:29; 1 Pet. 1:19; Rev. 5:6-9), and as seen in Christ as the ox to bear the responsibility and to labor faithfully for the accomplishing of God's will (Matt. 20:28; John 5:17; 6:38).

2. Through further growth in the divine life the believers in Christ are able to live on the earth a life that is useful for the fulfilling of God's will (cf. Rom. 5:17; 1 Cor. 3:2; Gal. 6:2; 1 Cor. 15:10, 58).

B. The human life is the highest created life, the life that can express God in His image and likeness and can exercise dominion for God:

1. Adam, the first man, typifies Christ (Rom.

5:14; 1 Cor. 15:45, 47; Psa. 8:4-8; Heb. 2:6-9)
as the center of God's creation (Col. 1:16-17),
as the Head of all creation (v. 15) and of all
men (1 Cor. 11:3), as God's expression in
God's image and likeness (Heb. 1:3; 2 Cor.
4:4; Col. 1:15), and as God's representative
to rule over all things created by God (Psa.
8:6-8; Matt. 28:18).

2. God's intention that man would express God
   in His image and represent God with His
   dominion is fulfilled not in Adam as the
   first man (1 Cor. 15:45a), the old man (Rom.
   6:6), but in Christ as the second man (1 Cor.
   15:47b), the new man (Eph. 2:15), comprising Christ Himself as the Head and the
   church as His Body (1:22-23; 1 Cor. 12:12;
   Col. 3:10-11).

3. It is fully fulfilled in the overcoming believers,
   who live Christ for His corporate expression
   (Phil. 1:19-26) and will have authority over
   the nations and reign as co-kings with Christ
   in the millennium (Rev. 2:26-27; 20:4, 6).

4. It will ultimately be fulfilled in the New
   Jerusalem, which will express God's image,
   having His glory and bearing His appearance (4:3a; 21:11, 18a), and also exercise
   God's divine authority to maintain God's
   dominion over the entire universe for eternity (v. 24; 22:5).

Morning Nourishment

Gen. But the earth became waste and emptiness, and
1:2-4 darkness was on the surface of the deep, and the
Spirit of God was brooding upon the surface of the
waters. And God said, Let there be light; and there
was light. And God saw that the light was good,
and God separated the light from the darkness.

[Genesis 1:2] is the first mentioning of the Spirit in the Bible.
The Spirit of God, as the Spirit of life (Rom. 8:2), came to brood
over the waters of death in order to generate life, especially
man (Gen. 1:26), for God's purpose. In spiritual experience, the
Spirit's coming is the first requirement for generating life (John
6:63a). (Gen. 1:2, footnote 5)

After the Spirit's brooding (Gen. 1:2b), the word of God
came to bring in the light (cf. Psa. 119:105, 130). In spiritual
experience, the coming of the word is the second requirement
for generating life (John 5:24; 6:63b), and the coming of the
light is the third requirement (Matt. 4:13-16; John 1:1-13).

The Spirit, the word, and the light were the instruments
used by God to generate life for the fulfillment of His purpose.
The Spirit, the word, and the light are all of life (Rom. 8:2; Phil.
2:16; John 8:12b). Christ as the Spirit is the reality of God
(Rom. 8:9-10; 2 Cor. 3:17; John 16:13-15); Christ as the Word is
the speaking of God (John 1:1; Heb. 1:2); and Christ as the light
is the shining of God (John 8:12a; 9:5). (Gen. 1:3, footnote 1)

The separation of the light from the darkness for the purpose
of discerning day from night (Gen. 1:5; cf. 2 Cor. 6:14b) is the
fourth requirement for generating life. (Gen. 1:4, footnote 1)

Today's Reading

Genesis 1, strictly speaking, is not a record of creation [but of
life]....God did not create the earth waste, but it became waste....
Due to the rebellion of Satan...recorded in Isaiah 14:9-14 and
Ezekiel 28:12-18,...the whole universe was judged by God, and
through that judgment the earth became waste and emptiness.

In Genesis 1:2 there are four words describing the desolation of the earth under God's judgment: *waste, emptiness, darkness,* and *deep.* The earth became waste and emptiness, and darkness was on the surface of the deep. On the surface of the earth was the deep, and on the surface of the deep was darkness. This tells us that there was no life, but death. The earth becoming waste and emptiness with darkness on the surface of the deep is a picture of death.

The word for *brood* [in verse 2] is the same word as *hovers* in Deuteronomy 32:11. This verse says that God is like an eagle who spreads his wings and hovers over his young. The Spirit of God was brooding, stretching out His wings, over the death situation for the purpose of producing life. The brooding of a hen over eggs is to produce some living things. In the Bible the Spirit of God is first mentioned as the brooding Spirit. This brooding of the Spirit indicates that Genesis 1 is not merely a record of God's creation but a record of life.

[In Genesis 1:3] light comes in to produce life. Where darkness is, there is death. Where light is, there is life. In Genesis 1 light came in mainly for life, not for creation. Genesis 1 is not mainly a record of creation but a record of life.…[In verse 4] the separation of the light from the darkness is for producing life. When we were saved, the divine light came into us, and that light did a separating, or dividing, work. The things of light were separated from the things of darkness. Light comes in for life, and this light divides, or separates, the positive things from the negative things. Verse 5 says, "God called the light Day, and the darkness He called Night. And there was evening and there was morning, one day."…The Bible reckons a day from the evening until the morning. The biblical way is better than the human way. The human way goes down from morning to evening, but the biblical way goes up from evening to morning. There was the evening, but now there is the morning. There was darkness, but now there is light. There was death, but now there is life. (*CWWL, 1969*, vol. 2, p. 390)

Further Reading: *CWWL, 1969*, vol. 2, *"The Crucial Revelation of Life in the Scriptures,"* ch. 1; *The Central Thought of God*, chs. 1-2

Enlightenment and inspiration: _____

_____

_____

_____

Morning Nourishment

Gen. And God made the expanse and separated the wa-
1:7-9 ters which were under the expanse from the waters
which were above the expanse, and it was so. And
God called the expanse Heaven. And there was
evening and there was morning, a second day. And
God said, Let the waters under the heavens be
gathered together into one place, and let the dry
land appear; and it was so.

The separating of the waters by producing an expanse between them, signifying, spiritually, the dividing of the heavenly
things from the earthly things through the work of the cross
(Col. 3:1-3; Heb. 4:12), was the fifth requirement for generating
life. (Gen. 1:6, footnote 2)

The appearing of the dry land is the sixth requirement for
generating life. This took place on the third day, corresponding
to the day of resurrection (1 Cor. 15:4). In the Bible the sea represents death and the land represents Christ (see footnote 7[1] in
Deut. 8) as the generating source of life. After the land appeared,
every kind of life—the plant life, the animal life, and even the
human life—was produced out of the land (Gen. 1:11-12, 24-27;
2:7). This typifies that the divine life with all its riches comes out
of Christ. On the third day Christ came out of death in resurrection to generate life (John 12:24; 1 Pet. 1:3) for the constituting of
the church. (Gen. 1:9, footnote 1)

Today's Reading

To divide light from darkness is rather objective; to divide the
waters above the expanse from the waters under the expanse is
more subjective. We need the second separation—dividing the
heavenly things from the earthly things (Col. 3:1-3). The waters
under the expanse represent the earthly things, while the waters
above the expanse represent heavenly things. Some things may
not be dark, but they are earthly, not heavenly.

The expanse is simply the atmosphere, the air surrounding the
earth. Without the atmosphere no life could ever be generated

upon the earth. There is no life on the moon because there is no expanse around the moon. God created the expanse surrounding the earth so that the earth may produce life. After being saved, we not only have the light within us, but also the air, the expanse. Something has come into us to separate the heavenly things from the earthly things, the things above which are acceptable to God from the things below which are not acceptable to Him. What is this? This is the dividing work of the cross. After we have been saved and have gone on with the Lord, we will experience the cross. The cross divides. It divides the natural things from the spiritual things, it divides the holy things from the common things, and it divides the heavenly things from the earthly things. Hebrews 4:12 tells us that the living Word can separate us to such an extent that our soul is divided from our spirit. I may say or do something good; yet that good word or deed does not have its source in the spirit, but in the soul. Morally speaking, ethically speaking, or humanly speaking, there is nothing wrong. But spiritually speaking, the source is not of God, not of the heavens. It is not of the spirit, but of the soul, of the earth. Thus, we need a further division: not only a separation between light and darkness, but also a discernment between the spirit (the things above) and the soul (the things beneath).

After the second day, we have the third day—the day of resurrection. On the third day, the day of resurrection, the dry land appeared under the expanse for generating life....In the whole Bible, the sea represents death and the earth represents Christ Himself. The Bible tells us that, eventually, after God has worked through many generations, the sea will be eliminated....In Jeremiah 5:22 we are told that God drew a line to limit the sea. Today, God is still working to eliminate the sea because in it there are demons. The sea represents something demonic, something devilish....In the new heavens and new earth there is only land, no sea (Rev. 21:1). The sea representing a main part of Satan's kingdom has been eliminated. Praise the Lord! (*Life-study of Genesis,* pp. 32-34)

Further Reading: Life-study of Genesis, msg. 3

Enlightenment and inspiration: _____

_____

_____

_____

Morning Nourishment

Gen. **And God called the dry land Earth, and the gather-**
1:10-11 **ing together of the waters He called Seas; and God**
saw that it was good. And God said, Let the earth
sprout grass, herbs yielding seed, *and* fruit trees
bearing fruit according to their kind with their
seed in them upon the earth; and it was so.

Dividing the land from the waters signifies separating life
from death. From the second day (Gen. 1:6-7) God began to work
to confine and limit the waters of death that covered the earth
(cf. Jer. 5:22). Eventually, when God's work is completed, in the
new heaven and new earth there will be no more sea (Rev. 21:1
and footnote 3). Furthermore, in the New Jerusalem there will be
no more night (Rev. 21:25 and footnote 2). This means that both
death and darkness will be eliminated. (Gen. 1:10, footnote 1)
  The countless varieties of the plant life typify the rich expression of the unsearchable riches of the life of Christ in their
beauty for man's sight (Gen. 2:9), in their fragrance (S. S. 1:12-
13), and in their nourishing man and animals (Gen. 1:29-30). The
trees (2:9; Exo. 15:23-25; S. S. 2:3…), the flowers (S. S. 1:14), and
the grains as food for man (John 6:9, 13) and as offerings to God
(Lev. 2:1-3, 14) are all types of Christ. (Gen. 1:11, footnote 1)

Today's Reading

The dry land appeared in order to produce life, to generate
life. On the third day, Christ came out of death. Christ came out
of death in resurrection just to generate life. Hallelujah!
  As we grow in the Lord, we learn how to discern light from
darkness, separate heavenly things from earthly things, and
divide life from death. In my speaking I may have nothing dark
and nothing earthly; yet I speak without life. I am devoid of life.
My speaking is genuine and proper, with nothing of darkness
and nothing worldly, but nevertheless is full of death. So, I must
pray, "Lord Jesus, drive away all the death waters within me
that the dry land may appear to produce life." In my speaking
there should be nothing of darkness, nothing of this earth, and

nothing of death. Within my speaking there must be the dry land that produces life.

In your family life, there may be nothing of darkness, nothing worldly, but also nothing of life. When someone comes into your home, he cannot see anything dark or worldly; neither can he see anything living. All that he can see there is death. But I hope that when I come to see you, I will see that everything is full of life. Christ, the dry land, is appearing in your home. Christ is manifested, producing life in your home.

The plant life on the land was generated. The lowest life, a life without consciousness, came into existence....If we talk to the grass or to the trees, the grass cannot understand and the trees will not react because they have no feeling, no consciousness. They have no emotion, thought, or will because they are lives without any consciousness. This is the lowest life.

When we received Christ into us, Christ appeared out of the death water within us. Christ appeared and now we have life, the generating of life. We are saved and we have life. At the time we were saved, we received life, but the life within us was very low. This is signified in the record of Genesis by the life of the grass, the life of the herbs, and the life of the fruit trees.

Even with the plant life there are three levels: grass, the lowest plant life; the herbs which yield seeds, a higher level; and the fruit trees, an even higher level.

When you became a Christian, you received life, but that life in you was very low. Perhaps the life within you is similar to grass: it is life and it grows; yet it is the lowest life....Although last week you might have been like the grass, today you have grown a little higher, and you have become the herb yielding the seed. I hope after two months, you will be a tree bringing forth fruit....But when you become a tree, do not become satisfied. This is not the last verse of chapter 1; it is something which happened on the third day. (*Life-study of Genesis,* pp. 34-35, 38-39)

Further Reading: Life-study of Genesis, msg. 4

Enlightenment and inspiration: _____

_____

_____

_____

Morning Nourishment

Gen. ...God said, Let there be light-bearers in the expanse
1:14-16 of heaven to separate the day from the night, and let
them be for signs and for seasons and for days and
years...and let them be...to give light on the earth; and
it was so. And God made the two great light-bearers,
the greater light-bearer to rule the day and the
lesser light-bearer to rule the night, and the stars.

According to the revelation of the whole Bible, light is for
life; light and life always go together (Psa. 36:9; Matt. 4:16;
John 1:4; 8:12; 1 John 1:1-7). The higher the light, the higher
the life. The indefinite light of the first day (Gen. 1:3) was sufficient for generating the lowest forms of life; the more solid and
more definite light from the light-bearers—the sun, the moon,
and the stars (v. 16; Psa. 136:7-9)—on the fourth day was necessary for producing the higher forms of life, including the
human life. This signifies that for our spiritual rebirth, the
light of the "first day" is sufficient; but for the growth in the
divine life unto maturity, more and stronger light, the light of
the "fourth day," is needed. (Gen. 1:14, footnote 1)

Today's Reading

Although light came in on the first day, it was not that solid,
not that strong. On the fourth day, not only the lights came, but
also the light-bearers—the sun, the moon, and the stars. These
are lights which are stronger, more solid, and more available.
This is the first requirement for the growth of life.

Suppose that you are not only the grass or the herb, but also
the tree. By this time you will receive more light....You need to receive some higher lights, some fuller lights, some richer, stronger,
and more available lights. First John 1:5-7 tells us that after we
are saved we need more light, that we need to walk in the light.

Genesis 1:14-19 [speaks about lights]...in a very definite
way—the sun, the moon, and the stars. In typology, the sun typifies Christ. Christ is our sun. Malachi 4:2 tells us that Christ is
the Sun of Righteousness and that there is healing in His wings.

His shining forth is the wings, and with this shining forth there is healing. The second half of this verse tells us that we all will grow up under the shining of Christ.

The moon is the church.…[In] Joseph's dream…the sun was his father, the moon his mother, and the stars his brothers [Gen. 37:9-11]. Based upon this fact, we may say that the church as the wife, the bride of Christ, may be typified by the moon.…The moon is an object that has no light in itself, but has the ability to reflect light.…The church was made in a way to reflect the light of Christ. Furthermore, the moon is able to reflect light only in the night time. Today, during the church age, it is the night time.… Although the church is really in a dark night (the local churches are lampstands shining in this dark night, Rev. 1:20), she can reflect the light of Christ. However, frequently the church (like the moon) is not very stable, coming up and going down. The church may be the full moon, the half moon, or the new moon.

We not only have the sun, the moon, but also the stars: not only Christ, the church, but also all the overcoming saints. Daniel 12:3 says that those who turn many to righteousness shine like the stars. If we are going to help people to be saved, if we are going to turn people from darkness to light, if we are going to recover all the backsliders, we must be the shining stars. Revelation 1:20 tells us that the churches are the lampstands shining in the darkness and that the angels (the living ones in the churches) are the shining stars. The Lord said that the saints are "the light of the world" (Matt. 5:14), and Paul said that the saints shine "as luminaries in the world" (Phil. 2:15).

The lights God made on the fourth day were established "to rule over the day and over the night" by their shining (Gen. 1:18a).…Where there is shining, there is ruling. Darkness brings in confusion, but light regulates. For the growth of life, we need the ruling and the regulating of the fourth-day lights. (*Life-study of Genesis*, pp. 39-41)

Further Reading: Life-study of Genesis, msg. 5

Enlightenment and inspiration: _____

_____

_____

_____

Morning Nourishment

Gen. **And God said, Let the waters swarm with swarms**
1:20-21 **of living animals, and let birds fly above the earth**
in the open expanse of heaven. And God created
the great sea creatures and every living animal that
moves, with which the waters swarmed, according
to their kind, and every winged bird according to
its kind; and God saw that it was good.

[Genesis 1:20 speaks of] the animal life with the lowest consciousness, corresponding to the first step in the believers'
growth in life (cf. 1 John 2:13). The animal life in the sea typifies
the riches of the life of Christ in the power that overcomes death
(signified by the salt water) in His living. Just as fish can live in
salt water without becoming salty, Christ and His believers, who
have the divine life, can live in the satanic world without being
"salted" by the world's corruption (cf. John 14:30; 17:15-16). The
animal life in the sea also shows the riches of Christ's life in feeding man with His riches (John 6:9a; 21:9). (Gen. 1:20, footnote 1)

The bird life is higher than the fish life. Fish can live in the
death waters, but birds can transcend the death waters. By
growing further in the divine life, the believers are able to transcend all the frustrations of the earth (cf. Isa. 40:31). The bird life
typifies the riches of the life of Christ as seen in His being the
eagle for carrying God's redeemed to His destination (Exo. 19:4;
Deut. 32:11-12; Rev. 12:14) and in His being the turtledoves or
pigeons for offering to God for the sins of God's people (Lev. 1:14;
5:7). (Gen. 1:20, footnote 2)

Today's Reading

Although every form of animal life has some level of consciousness, some lives are higher and others are lower. [In Genesis 1:20-
22] first, the fish are mentioned, the animal life with the lowest
consciousness....Suppose there are some goldfish swimming in
the water and we come near them. They will be frightened away.
However, if we scatter some food into the water and keep away, all
the fish will return. This life is higher than the tree life, higher

than the plant life (Ezek. 47:7, 9). Although it is not very high, it is higher. This is the first step of the growth of life.

The fish in the sea live in salt water. As a rule, salt water *God* does not grow anything; it kills, allowing nearly no plants to grow. Salt water kills life. Fish, however, can live in salt water. The water may be salty, but the fish will never be salty, unless they are dead. This is quite meaningful.

All of humanity, the entire human society, is like a great salt sea. Yet, we Christians are so living. We can be alive and live in such a society and not be salted by it. But once we are dead, we will become salty....Life repels every kind of salt from the dead sea....In the midst of an environment of death, this life can still survive. This is good; yet there is more.

After the fish, the birds, the fowl in the air, were created on the fifth day (Gen. 1:20-23). This is the higher life with the lower consciousness. The bird life is higher than the fish life. Fish can live in the death waters, but birds can transcend them. After you become a fish, you must grow until you are a bird. When your classmates come to you and say, "Let us go to the movies," you will soar. No one can touch you—you will be transcendent. You will not only repel the salt, but you will transcend it.

Every item mentioned in the first chapter of Genesis has a Bible verse signifying that it is a type. For instance, the Lord Jesus told Peter that he would be a fisher of men (Matt. 4:19). By this word, the Lord Jesus likened all people to fish in the sea. Also, we have Isaiah 40:31, which says that they who wait on the Lord shall be as the eagles, soaring and transcending. This is a higher life. Many can testify that often they were soaring. We can live in any kind of situation, but with a little more growth we not only survive in evil circumstances, we also transcend them. We fly away and nothing can touch us. Hallelujah!...This is the second step of the growth of life. This is wonderful, but there is still more. (*Life-study of Genesis*, pp. 41-43)

Further Reading: Life-study of Genesis, msg. 6

Enlightenment and inspiration: _____

_____

_____

_____

Morning Nourishment

Gen. **And God said, Let the earth bring forth living ani-**
1:24 **mals according to their kind, cattle and creeping**
 things and animals of the earth...and it was so.
26 **And God said, Let Us make man in Our image, ac-**
 cording to Our likeness; and let them have dominion
 over the fish of the sea and over the birds of heaven
 and over the cattle and over all the earth and over
 every creeping thing that creeps upon the earth.

The cattle and the animals on the land are a higher life with a higher consciousness than that of the fish and the birds, a life that can accomplish something on the earth. The animals and the cattle on the land typify the riches of the life of Christ as seen in Christ as the conquering lion (Rev. 5:5) to fight for God's economy, as seen in Christ as the sheep and oxen for offering to God for the fulfillment of God's full redemption (Lev. 1:2-3, 10;...Rev. 5:6-9), and as seen in Christ as the ox to bear the responsibility and to labor faithfully for the accomplishing of God's will (Matt. 20:28; John 6:38). Through further growth in the divine life the believers in Christ are able to live on the earth a life that is useful for the fulfilling of God's will (cf. 1 Cor. 3:2...). (Gen. 1:24, footnote 1)

Today's Reading

On the sixth day the higher life with the higher consciousness came into existence (Gen. 1:24-25)....Genesis 49:9 speaks about the lion, likening Judah to a lion which can do many things. First Samuel 6:7, 12a tells about two milch cows which were used to carry the cart with the ark. These verses show that both the beasts and the cattle can accomplish something on this earth.... This is the third step of the growth of life.

We need to go on to the last part of the sixth day...[on which] comes the life with the highest consciousness, the human life, a life which expresses the image of God and has dominion over all things for God. (*Life-study of Genesis*, pp. 43, 46)

Adam, the first man, typifies Christ (Rom. 5:14...) as the center of God's creation (Col. 1:16-17), as the Head of all creation (Col. 1:15) and of all men (1 Cor. 11:3), as God's expression in God's image and likeness (...Col. 1:15), and as God's representative to rule over all things created by God (Psa. 8:6-8...). (Gen. 1:26, footnote 2)

God's intention that man would express God in His image and represent God with His dominion is fulfilled not in Adam as the first man (1 Cor. 15:45a), the old man (Rom. 6:6), but in Christ as the second man (1 Cor. 15:47b and footnote 2), the new man (Eph. 2:15 and footnote 8), comprising Christ Himself as the Head and the church as His Body (Eph. 1:22-23; 1 Cor. 12:12 and footnote 2; Col. 3:10-11 and footnote 11[9]). It is fully fulfilled in the overcoming believers, who live Christ for His corporate expression (Phil. 1:19-26) and will have authority over the nations and reign as co-kings with Christ in the millennium (Rev. 2:26-27; 20:4, 6). It will ultimately be fulfilled in the New Jerusalem, which will express God's image, having His glory and bearing His appearance (Rev. 4:3a; 21:11, 18a), and also exercise God's divine authority to maintain God's dominion over the entire universe for eternity (Rev. 21:24; 22:5). (Gen. 1:26, footnote 5)

In His creation, God did not tell man to do anything. Man was created in the image of God and then committed by God with His divine authority. Man had a life with the image of God to express God and with the authority of God to represent God, not a life to do something or to work something for God. Many times when you meet some Christians, you have the sense that they are busy people working for God. They are diligent and faithful. But you do not sense the expression and the authority of God. On the other hand, with some saints, it seems that they are not so busy and not so diligent working for God, yet you sense the expression of God and the authority of God. You have the sense that God is with them. They are people full of the presence of God. Whenever you meet them, you sense the expression and the headship, the authority, of God. This is what God is after. (*The Central Thought of God,* pp. 22-23)

Further Reading: Life-study of Genesis, msgs. 7-8

Enlightenment and inspiration: _____

_____

_____

_____

Hymns, **#837**

1   We praise Thee, Lord, for Thy great plan
    That we Thy dwelling-place may be;
    Thou live in us, we filled with Thee,
    Thou in the Son expressed might be.

2   Though in Thine image made by Thee
    And given Thine authority,
    Yet we are only made of clay
    Without a trace of divinity.

3   When we receive Thee as our life,
    Thy nature we thru grace possess;
    Mingled together, we with Thee
    One Body glorious will express.

4   When flows Thy life thru all our souls,
    Filling, renewing every part,
    We will be pearls and precious stones,
    Changed to Thine image, as Thou art.

5   But, Lord, we fully realize
    These are not wrought men's praise to rouse,
    But as material to be built
    Together for Thy glorious house.

6   Here, Lord, we give ourselves to Thee;
    Receive us into Thy wise hands;
    Bend, break, and build together in Thee
    To be the house to meet Thy demands.

7   Break all the natural life for us,
    Deal Thou with each peculiar way,
    That we no more independent be
    But with all saints are one for aye.

8   Then we shall be Thy Bride beloved,
    Together in Thy chamber abide,
    Enjoy the fulness of Thy love.
    How Thou wilt then be satisfied!

Jer. 5:22

22 Do you not fear Me, declares Jehovah; Do you not tremble at My presence; Who have set the sand as a boundary for the sea By an eternal statute, so it cannot pass over it? Although its waves toss, they cannot prevail; Although they roar, they cannot pass over it.

Rev. 21:1, 25

1 And I saw a new heaven and a new earth; for the first heaven and the first earth passed away, and the sea is no more.

25 And its gates shall by no means be shut by day, for there will be no night there.

Gen. 2:9

9 And out of the ground Jehovah God caused to grow every tree that is pleasant to the sight and good for food, as well as the tree of life in the middle of the garden and the tree of the knowledge of good and evil.

Eph. 3:8-9

8 To me, less than the least of all saints, was this grace given to announce to the Gentiles the unsearchable riches of Christ as the gospel

9 And to enlighten all *that they may see* what the economy of the mystery is, which throughout the ages has been hidden in God, who created all things,

Footnotes: Genesis 1:10[1], 11[1]
Suggested Reading: Life Study of Genesis, #3, pp. 34-35 (Sections: (6) The Separation of the Earth From the Waters [paragraphs 2, 5-6]); Life Study of Genesis, #4, pp. 38-39 (Sections: (7) The Plant Life was Generated [paragraphs 1-4])
Crystallization Study of Genesis HWMR – Week 3— Day 3

Psa. 36:9

9 For with You is the fountain of life; In Your light we see light.

Matt. 4:16

16 The people sitting in darkness have seen a great light; and to those sitting in the region and shadow of death, to them light has risen."

John 1:4

4 In Him was life, and the life was the light of men.

1 John 1:5-7

5 And this is the message which we have heard from

Morning Watch

Genesis 1:3-26

3 And God said, Let there be light; and there was light.

4 And God saw that the light was good, and God separated the light from the darkness.

5 And God called the light Day, and the darkness He called Night. And there was evening and there was morning, one day.

6 And God said, Let there be an expanse in the midst of the waters, and let it separate the waters from the waters.

7 And God made the expanse and separated the waters which were under the expanse from the waters which were above the expanse, and it was so.

8 And God called the expanse Heaven. And there was evening and there was morning, a second day.

9 And God said, Let the waters under the heavens be gathered together into one place, and let the dry land appear; and it was so.

10 And God called the dry land Earth, and the gathering together of the waters He called Seas; and God saw that it was good.

11 And God said, Let the earth sprout grass, herbs yielding seed, and fruit trees bearing fruit according to their kind with their seed in them upon the earth; and it was so.

12 And the earth brought forth grass, herbs yielding seed according to their kind, and trees bearing fruit with their seed in them according to their kind; and God saw that it was good.

13 And there was evening and there was morning, a third day.

14 And God said, Let there be light-bearers in the expanse of heaven to separate the day from the night, and let them be for signs and for seasons and for days and years;

15 And let them be light-bearers in the expanse of heaven to give light on the earth; and it was so.

16 And God made the two great light-bearers, the greater light-bearer to rule the day and the lesser light-bearer to rule the night, and the stars.

17 And God set them in the expanse of heaven to give light on the earth

18 And to rule over the day and over the night and to separate the light from the darkness, and God saw that it was good.

19 And there was evening and there was morning, a fourth day.

20 And God said, Let the waters swarm with swarms of living animals, and let birds fly above the earth in

Composition for prophecy with main point and sub-points: _____

_____
_____
_____
_____
_____
_____
_____
_____
_____
_____
_____
_____
_____
_____
_____
_____
_____
_____
_____
_____
_____
_____
_____
_____
_____
_____
_____
_____
_____
_____
_____
_____
_____
_____

God Creating Man in His Own Image for His Expression

Scripture Reading: Gen. 1:26-27; Col. 1:15; 2 Cor. 3:18; Rom. 8:29; Rev. 21:11

Day 1 I. **"Let Us make man in Our image, according to Our likeness...And God created man in His own image; in the image of God He created him" (Gen. 1:26a, 27a):**

A. *Let Us make man* reveals that a council was held among the three of the Godhead regarding the creation of man (v. 26a):

1. The decision to create man was made in eternity past, indicating that the creation of man was for the eternal purpose of the Triune God (Eph. 3:9-11).

2. God's intention in creating man was to carry out His divine economy for the dispensing of Himself into man (1 Tim. 1:4; Rom. 8:11).

B. God created man in His own image, according to His likeness (Gen. 1:26a):

1. God's image, referring to God's inner being, is the expression of the inward essence of God's attributes, the most prominent of which are love (1 John 4:8), light (1:5), holiness (Rev. 4:8), and righteousness (Jer. 23:6).

2. God's likeness, referring to God's form (Phil. 2:6), is the expression of the essence and nature of God's person.

3. God's image and God's likeness should not be considered as two separate things (Gen. 1:26a):

a. Man's inward virtues, created in man's spirit, are copies of God's attributes and are the means for man to express God's attributes.

b. Man's outward form, created as man's body, is a copy of God's form.

  4. God created man to be a duplication of Himself so that man may have the capacity to contain God and express Him:

   a. All other living things were created "according to their kind" (vv. 11-12, 21, 24-25), but man was created according to God's kind (cf. Acts 17:28-29a).

   b. Since God and man are of the same kind, it is possible for man to be joined to God and to live together with Him in an organic union (John 15:5; Rom. 6:5; 11:17-24; 1 Cor. 6:17).

C. Christ the Son is "the image of the invisible God," "the effulgence of His glory and the impress of His substance"—the expression of what God is (Col. 1:15; Heb. 1:3):

  1. Christ the Son, as God's embodiment, is the image of the invisible God, the expression of the essence of God's attributes (Col. 2:9; 1:15; 2 Cor. 4:4; Heb. 1:3).

  2. Man was created according to Christ with the intention that Christ would enter into man and be expressed through man (Col. 1:27; Phil. 1:20-21a).

Day 2 D. God's purpose in the creation of man in His image and according to His likeness is that man would receive Him as life and express Him in all His attributes (Gen. 1:26-27; 2:9):

  1. God created man in His image and according to His likeness because His intention is to come into man and to be one with man (Eph. 3:17a).

  2. God created man in His own image so that through His economy man may receive His life and nature and thereby become His expression (1 Tim. 1:4; John 3:16; 2 Pet. 1:4; 2 Cor. 3:18).

  3. God created man in such a way that man has the capacity to contain God's love, light,

righteousness, and holiness (1 John 4:8; 1:5; Eph. 4:24; 5:2, 8-9).

4. Because we were created according to God's kind, our human virtues have the capacity to contain the divine attributes (2 Cor. 10:1; 11:10).

Day 3   E. For God to create man in His image means that God created man with the intention that man would become a duplicate of God, the reproduction of God, for His corporate expression; this reproduction makes God happy because it looks like Him, speaks like Him, and lives like Him (John 12:24; Rom. 8:29; Heb. 2:10; 1 John 3:1-2).

F. In the Bible there is a mysterious thought concerning the relationship between God and man (Gen. 1:26; Ezek. 1:26; 1 John 3:2b; Rev. 4:3a; 21:11b):

1. God's desire is to become the same as man is and to make man the same as He is (1 John 3:2b).

2. God's intention is to work Himself in Christ into us, making Himself the same as we are and making us the same as He is (Eph. 3:17a).

3. God's economy is to make Himself man and to make us, His created beings, God so that He is God "man-ized" and we are man "God-ized" (John 1:14; Rom. 1:3-4).

Day 4   G. The pronouns *them* in Genesis 1:26-28 and *their* in 5:2 indicate that Adam was a corporate man, a collective man, including all mankind:

1. God did not create many men; He created mankind collectively in one person, Adam.

2. God created such a corporate man in His image and according to His likeness so that mankind might express God corporately.

Day 5 **II. Christ's incarnation and God-man living fulfilled God's intention in His creation of man (1:26-27; John 1:1, 14; Luke 1:31-32, 35; 2:40, 52):**

A. The incarnation of Christ is closely related to God's purpose in the creation of man in His image and according to His likeness—that man would receive Him as life and express Him in His divine attributes (Gen. 1:26; 2:9; Acts 3:14a; Eph. 4:24).

B. The Lord Jesus was born of the human essence with the human virtues in order to uplift these virtues to such a standard that they can match God's attributes for His expression (Luke 1:35):

  1. As the One who was conceived of the divine essence with the divine attributes to be the content and reality of His human virtues, Christ fills the empty human virtues (Matt. 1:18, 20).

  2. The divine attributes fill, strengthen, enrich, and sanctify the human virtues for the purpose of expressing God in the human virtues.

C. When the Lord Jesus saves us, He comes into us as the One with the human virtues filled with the divine attributes (Luke 2:10-11, 25-32; 19:9-10):

  1. As the life-giving Spirit, He enters into us to bring God into our being and to fill our virtues with God's attributes (1 Cor. 15:45b; 6:17).

  2. Such a life saves us from within and uplifts our human virtues, sanctifying and transforming us (Rom. 5:10; 12:2).

Day 6 **III. In His incarnation Christ put on human nature and became in the likeness of men (Phil. 2:6-8) so that through His death and resurrection man may obtain God's eternal, divine life (1 Pet. 1:3; 1 John 5:11-12) and by that life be transformed and conformed to the image of Christ inwardly (2 Cor. 3:18; Rom. 8:29) and transfigured into the likeness of Christ's glorious body outwardly (Phil. 3:21); in this way we may be the same as Christ (1 John 3:2b)** and may express God with Him to the universe (Eph. 3:21):

A. By beholding the glory of the resurrected and ascended Lord with an unveiled face, we are "being transformed into the same image"—the image of the resurrected and glorified Christ (2 Cor. 3:18).

B. God has predestinated us to be conformed to the image of the firstborn Son of God; as the end result of transformation, conformation includes the changing of our inward essence and nature and also of our outward form so that we may match the glorified image of Christ (Rom. 8:29).

C. In Genesis 1:26 we see a corporate man created in God's image for His expression, and in Revelation 21 we see the New Jerusalem as the ultimate development and consummation of the image in Genesis 1:26; the city of God is the corporate expression of God, bearing the image of God and shining with the glory of God (Rev. 4:3; 21:11).

Morning Nourishment

Gen. **And God said, Let Us make man in Our image,**
1:26-27 **according to Our likeness; and let them have do-**
minion over the fish of the sea and over the birds of
heaven and over the cattle and over all the earth
and over every creeping thing that creeps upon
the earth. And God created man in His own image;
in the image of God He created him; male and
female He created them.

After God created [the plant life and the animal life], God still needed to create man as the highest created life to express Himself in His image and after His likeness. To accomplish this work, there is the need of the Triune God—the Father, the Son, and the Spirit—to work on man. This is fully proven by the following books of the whole Bible. (*Life-study of Genesis,* p. 62)

Let Us [in Genesis 1:26]...reveals that a council was held among the three of the Godhead regarding the creation of man. The decision to create man had been made by the Triune God in eternity past, indicating that the creation of man was for the eternal purpose of the Triune God (Eph. 3:9-11). God's intention in creating man was to carry out His divine economy for the dispensing of Himself into man (1 Tim. 1:4 and footnote 3, par. 1). This is fully unveiled in the following books of the Bible. (Gen. 1:26, footnote 1)

Today's Reading

God's image, referring to God's inner being, is the expression of the inward essence of God's attributes, the most prominent of which are love (1 John 4:8), light (1 John 1:5), holiness (Rev. 4:8), and righteousness (Jer. 23:6). God's likeness, referring to God's form (Phil. 2:6), is the expression of the essence and nature of God's person. Thus, God's image and God's likeness should not be considered as two separate things. Man's inward virtues, created in man's spirit, are copies of God's attributes and are the means for man to express God's attributes. Man's outward form, created as man's body, is a copy of God's form. Thus, God created man to be a duplication of Himself that man may have the

capacity to contain God and express Him. All the other living
things were created "according to their kind" (Gen. 1:11-12, 21,
24-25), but man was created according to God's kind (cf. Acts
17:28-29a). Since God and man are of the same kind, it is possible for man to be joined to God and to live together with Him in
an organic union (John 15:5; Rom. 6:5; 11:17-24; 1 Cor. 6:17).

Christ the Son, as God's embodiment (Col. 2:9), is the image of
the invisible God, the expression of the essence of God's attributes
(Col. 1:15; 2 Cor. 4:4; Heb. 1:3). Man was created according to Christ
with the intention that Christ would enter into man and be
expressed through man (Col. 1:27; Phil. 1:20-21a). Created man is
a living vessel, a container, to contain Christ (Rom. 9:21, 23; 2 Cor.
4:7). Eventually, in His incarnation Christ put on human nature
and became in the likeness of men (Phil. 2:6-8) so that through
His death and resurrection man may obtain God's eternal, divine
life (1 Pet. 1:3; 1 John 5:11-12) and by that life be transformed and
conformed to the image of Christ inwardly (2 Cor. 3:18; Rom. 8:29)
and transfigured into the likeness of Christ's glorious body outwardly (Phil. 3:21) that he may be the same as Christ (1 John
3:2b) and may express God with Him to the universe (Eph. 3:21).

Created man was a duplication of God in God's image and
likeness, but he did not have the reality of God or the life of God.
Thus, he still needed to receive God as his life by eating of the
tree of life so that he might have the reality of God to express
Him (Gen. 2:9 and footnote 2). (Gen. 1:26, footnote 3)

[According to Colossians 1:15] God is invisible. But the Son of
His love, who is the effulgence of His glory and the impress of His
substance (Heb. 1:3), is His image, expressing what He is. The
image here is not a physical form but an expression of God's
being in all His attributes and virtues (see footnote 6^2 in Phil. 2).
This interpretation is confirmed by Colossians 3:10 and 2 Corinthians 3:18. (Col. 1:15, footnote 1)

Further Reading: Life-study of Genesis, msg. 6; *Truth Lessons—
Level One,* vol. 1, lsn. 3

Enlightenment and inspiration: _____

_____
_____
_____

Morning Nourishment

Eph. **That Christ may make His home in your hearts**
3:17 **through faith...**

2 Cor. **But we all with unveiled face, beholding and re-**
3:18 **flecting like a mirror the glory of the Lord, are**
being transformed into the same image from glory
to glory, even as from the Lord Spirit.

God's purpose in the creation of man in His image and after His likeness was that man would receive Him as life and express Him in all His attributes.

If we have an all-inclusive view of the entire revelation in the Scriptures, both of the Old Testament and of the New Testament, we shall see that God designed man to be one with Him. God made this design in eternity past. It is a great matter that God designed man to be one with Him. Of course, in the Bible we cannot find the word *design* used with respect to man's being one with God. Nevertheless, if we have an all-inclusive view of the revelation in the holy Word, we shall see that in eternity past God designed man to be one with Him. (*Life-study of Luke*, pp. 483-484) *that's why He placed man in front of the tree of life.*

Today's Reading

We may use the designing and building of a house as an illustration of God's design concerning man. Before we build a house, we first need a design. Likewise, in the Bible we have both God's design and His building. Throughout the Scriptures we have a complete revelation of God's building. For His building God had a design. He designed to have man and that man should be one with Him. (*Life-study of Luke*, p. 484)

Now we need to ask why God created man in His own image, making man a copy of Himself, and why God created man with a spirit. God's economy is the answer to these questions. John 4:24 tells us that God is Spirit and that we must worship Him in spirit. Only the spirit can worship the Spirit. God created man in His own image, after His own likeness, with a spirit to worship Him and contact Him because of His divine economy. The divine economy is to carry out the divine dispensing of God into man. God created man in His own image…with a spirit so that He could dispense Himself into man. (*The Divine Economy,* p. 14)

God created us in His own image so that we would be His expression (Gen. 1:26). We are God's vessels to contain Him so that He may be expressed through us (Rom. 9:23). God chose us and predestinated us before the foundation of the world so that we would be conformed to the image of His Son (Eph. 1:4-5; Rom. 8:29). (*The Meaning of Human Life and a Proper Consecration,* p. 44)

Man was made in God's image. The man created by God, therefore, has love, light, and the capacity to be righteous and holy. Even though we are fallen, we still have in our fallen condition love, light, and the capacity to be right and to be holy like God. For God to create man in His own image means that God created man with the capacity to have His love, light, righteousness, and holiness. Human love, light, righteousness, and holiness are what we call the human virtues. These virtues were created by God….The human virtues were created by God to contain His attributes. Human love, light, righteousness, and holiness are created capacities to contain the divine love, light, righteousness, and holiness.

People everywhere agree that hating others is contrary to our conscience. Furthermore, it is also contrary to our conscience to lie, steal, and do things in darkness. Even an unsaved person may have the sense that it would be unrighteous to keep extra change given to him by mistake in a restaurant or store.

The point here is that man was made by God to have love and light and to walk righteously and to be holy. Man has these virtues because he was created in God's image, in the image of God's love, light, righteousness, and holiness. The human virtues created by God are the capacity to contain God's attributes. God created man in this way with the intention that man would take Him as the tree of life to be his life and content. (*Life-study of Luke,* pp. 489-490)

Further Reading: The Divine Economy, chs. 1-2; *The Meaning of Human Life and a Proper Consecration,* chs. 2-3

Enlightenment and inspiration: _____

_____

_____

_____

Morning Nourishment

John Truly, truly, I say to you, Unless the grain of wheat
12:24 falls into the ground and dies, it abides alone; but if
it dies, it bears much fruit.

Rom. Because those whom He foreknew, He also predesti-
8:29 nated *to be* conformed to the image of His Son, that
He might be the Firstborn among many brothers.

According to the Bible the image of God is related to His duplication. In Genesis 1 "image" is for God to be duplicated, to be "copied" in man. This means that man was created in such a way that he could become God's duplication, His copy....Since God created man for the purpose of man's becoming His duplication, and since this purpose is indicated by the use of the word *image,* we may go on to say that the word *image* implies the capacity to contain God. If man did not have the capacity to contain God, how could he become God's duplication, His copy? In order for man to be a copy of God, man must have the capacity or ability to contain what God is. (*Life-study of Luke,* p. 486)

Today's Reading

God's real hobby is to have His reproduction in many nations around the globe. Such a reproduction makes God happy because His reproduction looks like Him, speaks like Him, and lives like Him. God is in this reproduction, and His reproduction has His life, His nature, and His constitution. What a great matter this is! (*Life-study of 1 & 2 Chronicles,* p. 11)

In the Bible there is a mysterious thought concerning the relationship between God and man. God's desire is to become the same as man is and to make man the same as He is. This means that God's intention is to mingle Himself with man and thereby make Himself like man and make man like Him. The Lord Jesus is the God-man; He is the complete God and the perfect man. We may also say that He is the Man-God. The One whom we worship today is the Man-God. Furthermore, to be a man of God, as Moses was (Deut. 33:1; Josh. 14:6; Psa. 90, title), is to be a God-man, a man who is mingled with God. It is a delight to God that all His chosen and redeemed people would be God-men. (*Life-study of Ezekiel,* p. 124)

We need God to work Himself in Christ into us as our life, our nature, and our constitution. As a result, we are not simply a man according to God's heart—we are God in life and in nature but not in the Godhead....In order to accomplish this, God in Christ became a man and went through some processes that this man could be designated something divine. In resurrection He was designated the firstborn Son of God. In and through resurrection Christ, the firstborn Son of God, became the life-giving Spirit, who now enters into us to impart, to dispense, Himself as life into our being to be our inner constitution, to make us a God-man just like Him. He was God becoming man, and we are man becoming God in life and in nature but not in the Godhead. (*Life-study of 1 & 2 Samuel,* p. 168)

My burden is to show you clearly that God's economy and plan is to make Himself man and to make us, His created beings, "God," so that He is "man-ized" and we are "God-ized." In the end, He and we, we and He, all become God-men. Hence, it is not enough for us to be good men, spiritual men, or holy men. These are not what God is after. What God wants today is God-men. God does not expect us to improve ourselves, because God is not after our being good men. He wants us to be God-men. He is our life and everything to us for the purpose that we would express Him and live Him out.

We are like a picture, which has His image, but is without His life. After we are regenerated, this picture becomes the "real" person, having His life and nature, and being the same as He is. He is God "man-ized," and we are man "God-ized." In the end, the two become one, both being God-men. This is the divine revelation of the Bible. (*A Deeper Study of the Divine Dispensing,* p. 54)

Further Reading: Life-study of 1 & 2 Chronicles, msgs. 2, 4, 13; *Life-study of Ezekiel,* msg. 12

Enlightenment and inspiration: _____

_____

_____

_____

Morning Nourishment

1 Cor. So also it is written, "The first man, Adam, became a
15:45   living soul"; the last Adam *became* a life-giving Spirit.
Col.   Who is the image of the invisible God, the Firstborn
1:15   of all creation.

The pronouns *them* [in Genesis 1:26-28] and *their* in 5:2 indicate that Adam was a corporate man, a collective man, including
all mankind. God did not create many men; He created mankind
collectively in one person, Adam. God created such a corporate
man in His image and according to His likeness so that mankind
might express God corporately. (Gen. 1:26, footnote 4)

Today's Reading

On the sixth day God created the cattle and the beasts of the
earth. This is the life that can do something for man. The life of
a dog is much stronger than that of a fish. Then there is the
highest life among the creatures, which is the human life. This
is a life that not only can live in death, be transcendent, work
for God, and do the will of God but also can express and represent God. This is a life with the image of God and the authority
of God. It is at this point that God rested.

The completion of God's work is a life with His image and His
authority. We may have thought that God rested because He
had finished His work. But as long as there is not a life with the
image and authority of God, there is no rest for God. (*The Central Thought of God,* p. 17)

In the Bible Adam as the first man is a type of the Christ who
was to come (Rom. 5:14). As a type of Christ, Adam prefigured
Christ. Whatever purpose God had for Adam and whatever work
He did in Adam were to be carried out in and through Christ.

In God's creation Adam was the center of all creation. God
first established the heavens and prepared the earth, and then
He created man. He first made the light, the expanse, and the
land, and then He created the grass, the herbs, the trees, the
fish, the birds, the cattle, the beasts, and the creeping things.
Eventually, He created Adam. Thus we see that the heavens are

for the earth, and the earth with the different kinds of living things is for man. Therefore, man is the center of God's creation. This is a type of Christ as the real center of God's creation, because in Him, through Him, and unto Him all things were created, the things in the heavens and on the earth, the visible and the invisible, whether thrones, lordships, rulers, or authorities.

Adam was created as the head of the human race, and the human race was the center of God's creation. Therefore, Adam was the head of God's creation. This is a type of Christ as the Head of all God's creation.

Adam was created in God's image and according to God's likeness (Gen. 1:26). This typifies that Christ bears God's image and likeness. Colossians 1:15 says that Christ "is the image of the invisible God." God is invisible. But Christ, who is the effulgence of His glory and the impress of His substance (Heb. 1:3), is His image, expressing what He is.

After the creation of Adam, God wanted man to have dominion over all the living created things in the seas, in the air, and on the earth (Gen. 1:26, 28). God wanted the man whom He had created to be His representative to execute His authority and rule for Him on the earth. Therefore, man was not only created to express God but also given the authority to represent God to rule over all. This is a type of Christ as God's expression and also as God's representative. Christ as God's Anointed was anointed and commissioned by God for the carrying out of God's purpose in dealing with God's enemy to recover the enemy-usurped earth and bring in God's authority.

Adam was the first ancestor of the human race. When he was created, the entire human race, which was included in him, was created by God (Gen. 1:26). Thus, he became the head of all men. This is a type of Christ as the head of every man (1 Cor. 11:3). (*Truth Lessons—Level Three*, vol. 1, pp. 19-21)

Further Reading: The Central Thought of God, chs. 1-2; Truth Lessons—Level Three, vol. 1, lsn. 2

Enlightenment and inspiration: _____

_____

_____

_____

Morning Nourishment

Luke   And behold, you will conceive in *your* womb and
1:31-32 bear a son, and you shall call His name Jesus. He
will be great and will be called Son of the Most
High...

Rom.   For if we, being enemies, were reconciled to God
5:10   through the death of His Son, much more we will
be saved in His life, having been reconciled.

God's purpose in creating man was that man would be His duplication in order to express Him. In order for this purpose to be carried out, it is necessary for man to receive God and contain Him as the tree of life. However, Adam, the man created by God, failed in God's purpose and damaged God's design. Thousands of years later, the Man-Savior came to fulfill God's purpose in creating man.

Through the incarnation of Christ, God in the Son became a man. What a great matter this is! God had created man with a purpose according to His design, but man failed Him in His purpose and destroyed His design. Instead of creating another man, God Himself came to be the second Man (1 Cor. 15:47). God came to be the second Man not in the Father nor in the Spirit but in the Son. (*Life-study of Luke*, pp. 491-492)

Today's Reading

A crucial matter concerning the God-man is that He lived a human life filled with the divine life as its content....[The Gospel of Luke] is a revelation of the God-man who lived a human life filled with the divine life as its content. As the One who lived such a life, the Man-Savior had the divine nature with the divine attributes, that is, with the divine love, light, righteousness, and holiness. The divine nature with its attributes was expressed in the Man-Savior's human nature with all the human virtues. (*Life-study of Luke*, p. 492)

When we realize that we are God-men, we will say, "Lord, You are the first God-man, and we are the many God-men following You. You lived a human life, not by Your human life but by God's divine life to express Him. His attributes became Your virtues.

You were here on this earth dying every day. You were crucified to live. Lord, You are my life today and You are my person. You are just me. I therefore must die. I need to be conformed to Your death. I have to be crucified to die every day to live a God-man's life, a human life yet not by my human life but by the divine life, with Your life and Your nature as my constitution to express You in Your divine attributes, which become my human virtues." This makes us not just a Christian or a believer in Christ but a God-man, one kind with God. This is the highest point of God's gospel. (*Life-study of 1 & 2 Chronicles,* pp. 27-28)

The Man-Savior was incarnated in order to uplift the human virtues to the highest standard, to the standard that matches God's attributes for the expression of God. Because our virtues were damaged and deformed, they could not match God's attributes. But the uplifted human virtues can match God's attributes. The Man-Savior was born of the human essence with the human virtues in order to uplift these virtues to such a standard that they can match God's attributes for His expression.

Christ fills the empty human virtues....We may not have the concept that Christ's incarnation was to fill, strengthen, and enrich the human virtues....The Man-Savior's incarnation caused the empty human virtues to be filled, strengthened, and enriched with the divine attributes.

In order to save us, He, the very God, came into man, bringing God's attributes into man's virtues. While He was on earth, He lived the life of a God-man, with the divine attributes filling His human virtues. Eventually, He died on the cross and was resurrected. In His resurrection He became the life-giving Spirit (1 Cor. 15:45). Now as the life-giving Spirit He enters into us to bring God into our being and to fill our virtues with God's attributes. In this way we are being saved day by day. We are being saved in the way of the Lord's restoring, His transforming. (*Life-study of Luke,* pp. 505, 498-499, 507)

Further Reading: Life-study of Luke, msgs. 56-59

Enlightenment and inspiration: _____

_____

_____

_____

Morning Nourishment

Rev. And He who was sitting was like a jasper stone and
4:3 a sardius in appearance, and *there was* a rainbow
around the throne like an emerald in appearance.
21:11 Having the glory of God. Her light was like a most precious stone, like a jasper stone, as clear as crystal.

The goal of transformation is to be "transformed into the
same image" of the resurrected and glorified Christ [2 Cor. 3:18].
To be transformed to have the same image as Christ means that
we are gradually being conformed to the resurrected and glorified Christ, to be made the same as He (Rom. 8:29).

When we behold and reflect the glory of the Lord, the Lord
infuses and dispenses into us the elements of what He is and
what He has done. Through His life power and by His life essence,
we are gradually transformed metabolically to have His life shape,
and through the renewing of our mind, we are gradually transfigured into His image. (*Truth Lessons—Level Three*, vol. 3, p. 33)

Today's Reading

As the seed of a carnation grows by its life essence and
through its life power, it takes on a characteristic shape. The
divine life is the same. This life has an essence, power, and
shape. The shape of the divine life is the image of Christ. Therefore, when we grow by the essence of Christ's life and through
the power of His life, we are gradually transformed into
Christ's image, that is, into the image of the resurrected and
glorified Christ. (*Truth Lessons—Level Three*, vol. 3, p. 33)

With His firstborn Son as the base, pattern, element, and
means, God is producing many sons, and the many sons who are
produced are the many believers who believe into God's firstborn Son and are joined to Him as one. They are exactly like Him
in life and nature, and, like Him, they have both humanity and
divinity. They are His increase and expression in order that they
may express the eternal Triune God for eternity. The church
today is a miniature of this expression (Eph. 1:23), and the New
Jerusalem in eternity will be the ultimate manifestation of this

expression (Rev. 21:11).

God has predestinated us not simply that we may be sanctified, spiritual, and victorious but that we may be fully conformed to the image of His Son. This is our destiny, determined by God in eternity past. Conformation is the end result of transformation. It includes the changing of our inward essence and nature, and it also includes the changing of our outward form, that we may match the glorified image of Christ, the God-man. He is the prototype, and we are the mass reproduction. (*The Conclusion of the New Testament,* pp. 3081-3082)

In Revelation God sitting on the throne looks like jasper (4:3). Then in 21:18 John tells us that the wall of the city was made of jasper. These two verses tell us that the New Jerusalem will look like God. The city will be a corporate expression of God.

That God will have a corporate expression is also indicated in His creation of man. Before the ages God predestinated us unto sonship. Then He created man in His own image, according to His predestination, with the intention that one day this created man would be His corporate expression. That day is not here yet. When the four dispensations are over—the dispensations of the Patriarchs, of the law, of grace, and of the kingdom—God's work of conforming us to the image of the Firstborn will be completed. Then we will be a living corporate entity, bearing the image of God.

The New Jerusalem is the aggregate of all the sons together as a corporate expression. It is a composition of all the dear saints redeemed by God in all the dispensations, both of the Old and of the New Testaments. They together will be the components of this holy city, the aggregate of the divine sonship, expressing God corporately to fulfill His heart's desire, as indicated in His creating man in His own image. Revelation 21 and 22 are the fulfillment of Genesis 1:26—God having a man in His image. (*The Basic Revelation in the Holy Scriptures,* p. 144)

Further Reading: Truth Lessons—Level Three, vol. 3, lsns. 43-44;
The Central Line of the Divine Revelation, msgs. 5-6

Enlightenment and inspiration: _____

_____

_____

_____

Hymns, #1097

1   O Lord, our Lord, how excellent
    Thy name in all the earth!
  Let every people, tribe, and tongue
    Proclaim its boundless worth.
  Out of the mouth of little ones
    Thou hast established praise,
  That Thou may still Thine enemy
    And swiftly end his days.

2   When we the universe behold,
    The work of Thy great hand —
  The sun, the moon, and all the stars
    By lofty wisdom planned;
  O what is man that Thou should'st care
    That Thou should'st mindful be?
  The son of man Thou visitest
    In Thine economy.

3   O Jesus Lord, Thou art that man,
    The One who joined our race,
  Who put upon Himself the flesh
    And took a lower place.
  But now with glory Thou art crowned,
    With sovereignty complete.
  Now through Thy Body Thou dost rule
    With all beneath Thy feet.

4   Thine incarnation, rising too,
    And Thy transcendency,
  Thy Lordship, Headship, kingdom full,
    And Body here we see.
  By all these steps of work divine
    Thou hast established praise.
  With overflowing hearts to Thee
    Our joyful voice we raise.

5   Oh, soon that blessed day shall come —
    All tongues these words shall peal!
But in the local churches now
    We have a foretaste real.
O Lord, our Lord, how excellent
    Thy name in all the earth!
Let every people, tribe, and tongue
    Proclaim its boundless worth.

Composition for prophecy with main point and sub-points: _____

_____

_____

_____

_____

_____

_____

_____

_____

_____

_____

_____

_____

_____

_____

_____

_____

_____

_____

_____

_____

_____

_____

_____

_____

Dominion—Subduing the Enemy, Recovering the Earth, and Exercising God's Authority over the Earth

Scripture Reading: Gen. 1:26-28; Matt. 6:9-10, 13; 1 Cor. 15:47; Eph. 2:15; Rev. 11:15

Day 1   I. **God created a corporate man not only to express Him but also to represent Him by having dominion over all things (Gen. 1:26, 28):**

A. The revelation of the Bible is that the Triune God created man in His image and with His dominion to express Him and represent Him (v. 26).

B. God in His Divine Trinity created a singular man in His own image, and He committed to this man dominion over all the earth; the more we experience and enjoy the Triune God, the more we will grow in the reality of the divine image and the divine dominion (vv. 27-28; 2 Cor. 13:14; Eph. 3:14-17).

II. **God's intention in giving man dominion is to subdue God's enemy, Satan, who rebelled against God (Gen. 1:26, 28):**

A. The creeping things that creep upon the earth typify Satan, the serpent, and his angels, as well as the demons, who follow Satan (v. 26; 3:1, 14; Rev. 12:4, 7, 9; Matt. 25:41; cf. Luke 10:19).

B. *Subdue* in Genesis 1:28 implies that a war is raging on earth between God and His enemy, Satan; whoever gains the earth will have the victory.

C. God has a problem, and this problem is Satan, the archangel who rebelled against God and became His enemy in the universe and especially on the earth (Isa. 14:12-14; Ezek. 28:12-18):

1. According to Genesis 3:1, Satan as God's enemy hid himself in the serpent, one of the creeping things on the earth.

2. In order to subdue His enemy and thus solve His problem, God gave man authority to rule over all things created by God (1:26).

3. Man especially must rule over the earth and even subdue the earth because the earth has been usurped by God's rebellious enemy (v. 28).

4. God needs man to exercise His authority over all the creeping things, and God needs man to subdue and conquer the rebellious earth so that God may recover the earth for His kingdom (Matt. 6:9-10).

Day 2

D. God wants to use man to deal with His enemy, and He created man for this purpose; God wants His creature *man* to deal with His fallen creature *Satan* (Gen. 1:28).

E. "If man has not restored the earth from the hand of Satan, he has not yet achieved God's purpose in creating him...Dealing with Satan is for the benefit of God...Dealing with Satan satisfies God's need" (*The Glorious Church*, p. 11).

III. **God's intention in giving man dominion is to recover the earth (v. 28):**

A. God created man with the intention of recovering the earth for Himself (v. 26):

1. Man was created by God to have dominion over the earth, to subdue it, to conquer it, and thereby recover the earth for God (vv. 26, 28).

2. God wants to regain the earth; the earth has become a crucial place, a place that Satan wants to hold and a place that God wants to regain.

3. Man is commissioned to be fruitful and multiply, to fill the earth, and to subdue it (v. 28).

B. The Lord's name must be sanctified on earth and become excellent in all the earth (Matt. 6:9-10; Psa. 8:1, 9).

C. During the millennium the earth will become

the kingdom of God, and in eternity the New Jerusalem will come down out of heaven to the new
earth (Rev. 11:15; 21:1-2).

Day 3 **IV. God's intention in giving man dominion is to
exercise God's authority over the earth in
order that the kingdom of God may come to
the earth, the will of God may be done on
earth, and the glory of God may be manifested on earth (Matt. 6:10, 13b):**

A. We need to exercise God's authority so that the
kingdom of God may come to the earth (v. 10):

1. The genuine church is the kingdom of God
in this age (16:18-19; 18:17-18; 13:44-46;
Rom. 14:17; 1 Cor. 4:20; Eph. 2:19; Col. 4:11;
Rev. 1:4-6).

2. The church brings in the kingdom; the work
of the church is to bring in the kingdom of
God (Matt. 6:10; 12:22-29; Rev. 11:15; 12:10):

a. The church was brought into being for
the purpose of bringing in the kingdom
(Matt. 16:18-19; 18:17-18; Rev. 1:6, 9;
11:15).

b. The church should pray with authority
to bring in the kingdom of God (Matt.
6:10).

B. We need to exercise God's authority so that the
will of God may be done on earth (v. 10):

1. God is a God of purpose, having a will of His
own pleasure, and He created all things for
His will so that He might accomplish and
fulfill His purpose (Rev. 4:11; Eph. 3:9-11;
Col. 1:9).

2. The kingdom is absolutely a matter of God's
will and completely fulfills God's will; in
fact, the kingdom is God's will (Matt. 6:10).

3. We need to pray for the Father's will to be
done on earth as in heaven; this is to bring
the kingdom of the heavens to the earth
(v. 10).

Day 4   C. We need to exercise God's authority so that the glory of God may be manifested on the earth (v. 13):

1. God is a God of glory; glory is the expression of God, God expressed (Acts 7:2; Eph. 1:17; 3:14, 16, 21; Rev. 21:10-11).

2. The kingdom of God is the realm in which God exercises His power so that He can manifest His glory (Matt. 6:10, 13).

V. **God's intention that man would express God in His image and represent God with His authority is fulfilled in Christ as the second man and in the corporate one new man (1 Cor. 15:47; Eph. 2:15; 1:22-23; 1 Cor. 12:12; Col. 3:10-11):**

Day 5   A. Christ is not only the last Adam but also the second man (1 Cor. 15:45, 47):

1. The first Adam is the beginning of mankind; the last Adam is the ending (v. 45).

2. As the first man, Adam is the head of the old creation, representing it in creation; as the second man, Christ is the Head of the new creation, representing it in resurrection (vv. 45, 47).

3. We believers were included in the first man by birth and became part of the second man by regeneration; our believing into Christ has transferred us out of the first man into the second (Rom. 5:12-21).

B. The church is the one new man, which is corporate and universal, created of two peoples, the Jews and the Gentiles, and composed of all the believers, who, though they are many, are one new man in the universe (Eph. 2:15):

1. God created man as a collective entity (Gen. 1:26):

    a. The corporate man created by God was damaged through man's fall; hence, there was the need for God to produce a new man.

b. The producing of the new man was accomplished through Christ's abolishing
in His flesh the ordinances and through
His creating the new man in Himself
(Eph. 2:15).

Day 6
2. God's creation of man in Genesis 1 is a picture of the new man in God's new creation;
this means that the old creation is a figure,
a type, of the new creation (Eph. 2:15; 4:24):

a. Eventually, the church as the one new
man is the corporate man in God's intention, and this new man will fulfill the
twofold purpose of expressing God and
dealing with God's enemy.

b. God's intention is to regenerate many
members of the one new man, who are
the many members of the one Body of
Christ (1 Cor. 12:27).

c. As the church, the corporate man in
God's eternal purpose, we express God
and we represent Him to subdue the
earth and to conquer His enemy (Col.
3:10).

Morning Nourishment

Gen. And God said, Let Us make man in Our image, ac-
1:26 cording to Our likeness; and let them have dominion
over the fish of the sea and over the birds of heaven
and over the cattle and over all the earth and over
every creeping thing that creeps upon the earth.
28 And God blessed them; and God said to them, Be
fruitful and multiply, and fill the earth and subdue
it, and have dominion...

God created a corporate man not only to express Himself
with His image but also to represent Him by exercising His
dominion over all things. God's intention in giving man dominion is (1) to subdue God's enemy, Satan, who rebelled against
God; (2) to recover the earth, which was usurped by Satan; and
(3) to exercise God's authority over the earth in order that the
kingdom of God may come to the earth, the will of God may be
done on the earth, and the glory of God may be manifested on
the earth (Matt. 6:10, 13b). (Gen. 1:26, footnote 5)

Today's Reading

In Genesis 1:26 and 27 the word *man* in Hebrew is singular.
This indicates that the one God in His three persons created a
singular man in His own image, and He committed to this man
His dominion over all the earth. This one sentence encompasses
the divine revelation in the entire Bible, for the revelation of the
Bible is that the Triune God created a man in His image and
with His dominion to express Him and represent Him.

Through the enjoyment of the Triune God, day by day we are
growing in the reality of the divine image and the reality of
the divine dominion. The more we grow in Christ, the more we
have God's image, and the more we have God's authority. When
people come into the church meetings, they can touch the reality
of Christ in the flow of the Spirit, and they can see the expression of God and sense the subduing and conquering by the exercise of the divine authority. (*CWWL, 1970*, vol. 1, pp. 94, 106)

What was God's intention in giving man dominion?...The first aspect of God's intention is to deal with His enemy, to deal with Satan typified by the creeping things (Gen. 1:26). In the Bible, the creeping things are demonic, devilish, and satanic....Four living creatures, representing all creation, are present before the throne of God—the eagle, the ox, the lion, and the man. No creeping things such as serpents or scorpions are represented before God. (*Life-study of Genesis,* p. 79)

[In Genesis 1:26 *creeping thing* typifies] Satan, the serpent (3:1, 14; Rev. 12:9), and his angels (Matt. 25:41; Rev. 12:4a, 7b), as well as the demons who follow Satan (cf. Luke 10:19). (Gen. 1:26, footnote 6)

Subdue [in Genesis 1:28] implies that a war is raging on earth between God and His enemy, Satan. Whoever gains the earth will have the victory. (Gen. 1:28, footnote)

God gave created man dominion so that man could represent God by exercising His authority over all the things on the earth that were created by God. God is the Creator, but He does not want to rule over the earth by Himself directly. He gave dominion to man so that man could rule over all things on the earth....If we read the Bible carefully, we will see that God has a problem, and this problem is Satan, the archangel who rebelled against God and became His enemy in the universe and especially on the earth (Isa. 14:12-14; Ezek. 28:12-18). According to Genesis 3:1, Satan as God's enemy hid himself in the serpent, one of the creeping things on the earth. In order to subdue His enemy and thus solve His problem, God gave man the authority to rule over all the things created by God. Man especially must rule over the earth and even subdue the earth because the earth has been usurped by God's rebellious enemy. Thus, God needs man to exercise His authority over all the creeping things, and God needs man to subdue and conquer the rebellious earth so that God may recover the earth for His kingdom.

The enemy Satan is powerful, but we have the authority to stop him. (*CWWL, 1970,* vol. 1, pp. 97-99)

Further Reading: CWWL, 1970, vol. 1, pp. 94-107; *The Vision of God's Building,* ch. 1

Enlightenment and inspiration: _____

_____

_____
_____

Morning Nourishment

Psa. **O Jehovah our Lord, how excellent is Your name in**
8:1-2 **all the earth, You who have set Your glory over the**
heavens! Out of the mouths of babes and sucklings
You have established strength because of Your ad-
versaries, to stop the enemy and the avenger.

God wants to use man to deal with His enemy, and He created man for this purpose. God wants the creature to deal with
the creature. He wants His creature *man* to deal with His fallen
creature *Satan* in order to bring the earth back to God. The man
whom He created is being used by Him for this purpose.
(*CWWN*, vol. 34, "The Glorious Church," p. 10)

Today's Reading

If man has not restored the earth from the hand of Satan, he
has not yet achieved God's purpose in creating him. Saving souls
is often only for the welfare of man, but dealing with Satan is for
the benefit of God. Saving souls solves man's need, but dealing
with Satan satisfies God's need. (*CWWN*, vol. 34, p. 11)

The second aspect of God's intention in giving man dominion
is to recover the earth (Gen. 1:26-28). Man is to have dominion
over the earth, to subdue it, and to conquer it. To conquer the
earth means that the enemy is there already, that a war is
raging. Therefore, we must fight and conquer.

God wants to regain the earth. The earth has become a crucial place, a place that Satan wants to hold and a place that God
wants to regain. The battle is over the earth. Whoever gains the
earth is the winner. If Satan can keep the earth under his hand,
he has the victory. If God can regain the earth, He will have the
victory. The Lord Jesus has not returned because the earth is
still so much under Satan's usurping. This is why God needs the
church. The church must fight the battle to regain the earth, if
not the whole earth, at least some stepping stones, some outpost
for the Lord Jesus to put His feet upon. The earth is crucial.

This point has been fully proved by Psalm 8. Psalm 8 begins
by saying, "O Jehovah our Lord, how excellent is Your name in

all the earth!" It also ends the same way. There is no doubt that the Lord's name is excellent in the heavens, but, in a sense, the name of the Lord is not excellent on this earth. His name is not excellent among so many of the fallen people. We need to pray, "Your name be sanctified" (Matt. 6:9). Oh, the Lord's name must be sanctified on this earth. The problem is not in the heavens; the problem is here on earth.

God desires that His kingdom come to this earth and that His will be done on earth (Matt. 6:10). Now we can understand the prayer which the Lord Jesus established. He said, "Your name be sanctified; Your kingdom come." Certainly this means to come from the heavens to the earth. The prayer continues, "Your will be done, as in heaven, so also on earth." God's will is now being done in heaven. But on the earth there are many frustrations, hindering God's will from being done. We must pray, "Let Your name be sanctified; let Your kingdom come; let Your will be done, as in heaven, so on earth." We must fight to recover the earth.

At the time of the millennium, the earth will become the kingdom of God. This is revealed in Revelation 11:15. When the Lord Jesus comes to inaugurate the millennium, the whole earth will become the kingdom of God. Then the earth will be regained by God.

In eternity, God's habitation will come down from heaven to the new earth (Rev. 21:1-2). Many Christians dream of going to heaven. That is a good dream and, undoubtedly, all of us will be there. However, God desires to come down to earth. We like the heavens, but God likes the earth. We are going up, and He is coming down. Hallelujah! Let me tell you the truth: when we get to heaven, the Lord will say, "Children, let us go down. Let us go down to take over the earth." In eternity, the heavens will not be God's habitation. God's habitation will be the New Jerusalem, and the New Jerusalem will come down from the heavens to the new earth. This proves that God's desire is to possess the earth. (*Life-study of Genesis,* pp. 81-82)

Further Reading: CWWN, vol. 34, "The Glorious Church," ch. 1

Enlightenment and inspiration: _____

_____

_____

_____

Morning Nourishment

Matt. **Your kingdom come; Your will be done, as in heaven,**
6:10 **so also on earth.**
16:18-19 **...Upon this rock I will build My church, and the
gates of Hades shall not prevail against it. I will give
to you the keys of the kingdom of the heavens, and
whatever you bind on the earth shall have been
bound in the heavens, and whatever you loose on
the earth shall have been loosed in the heavens.**

The third aspect of God's intention in giving man dominion is to
bring in [and] to exercise God's authority over the earth. Man must
exercise God's authority in order that the kingdom of God may
come to earth, that the will of God may be done on earth, and that
the glory of God may be manifested on earth. All of this will be on the
earth. God will never be satisfied to have His kingdom only in the
heavens. Neither will He be happy to have His will done only in
the heavens nor to see His glory expressed only in the heavens. He
wants all these things to happen on the earth. This is the responsibility of the church today. In the church we have the kingdom of
God. In the church the will of God is done. In the church the glory
of God is expressed. Hallelujah! We have a foretaste. Now we can
see why God gave man dominion over everything in the seas, in the
air, and on the earth. God's intention is to eliminate the enemy, regain the earth, and manifest His glory. (*Life-study of Genesis,* p. 83)

Today's Reading

The Lord said in Matthew 16 that the gates of Hades shall not
overcome the built-up church (v. 18). Following this, "the kingdom
of the heavens" (v. 19) is mentioned. The interchangeable use of
"the kingdom of the heavens" in this verse with "My church" in the
previous verse proves strongly that the genuine church is the
kingdom of the heavens in this age. Hence, the church, the kingdom of God, and the dealing with Satan are all linked together.
Where the church is, Satan is overcome, and the kingdom of God
is brought in. (*Salvation in Life in the Book of Romans,* p. 54)

"Your kingdom come!" This is not only a desire of the church, but also a responsibility of the church. The church should bring in God's kingdom. In order to bring in God's kingdom, the church has to pay the price to be restricted by heaven and come under heaven's rule. It has to be the outlet for heaven, and it has to allow heaven's authority to be expressed on earth.

A prayer with authority has the position of being in the heavenlies as its basis. Since the church is in the heavenlies with Christ, it can pray with authority. (*CWWN*, vol. 22, pp. 164, 195)

The basis of God's work in creation was God's will and plan (Eph. 1:10-11). Revelation 4:11 says that all things were created according to God's will. God is a God of purpose, having a will of His own pleasure. He created all things for His will that He might accomplish and fulfill His purpose. God has a will, and according to that will He conceived His plan. Then according to that will and plan, He created all things so that He may have the church. (*The Conclusion of the New Testament*, p. 2056)

Although the kingdom is here in the church life today, the manifestation of the kingdom is yet to come [Matt. 6:10]. Thus, we must pray for the coming of the kingdom. This matter of the kingdom is clearly related to God the Son....Following the rebellion of Satan (Ezek. 28:17; Isa. 14:13-15), the earth fell into the usurping hand of Satan. Thus, the will of God could not be done on earth as in heaven. Hence, God created man with the intention of recovering the earth for Himself (Gen. 1:26-28). After the fall of man, Christ came to bring the heavenly rule to earth so that the earth might be recovered for God's right, that the will of God might be done on earth as in heaven....The kingdom people must pray for this until the earth is fully recovered for God's will in the coming kingdom age.

When the Father's name is sanctified, the Son's kingdom has come, and the Spirit's will is done on earth as in heaven, that will be the time of the manifestation of the kingdom. (*Life-study of Matthew*, pp. 266-267)

Further Reading: Life-study of Matthew, msg. 21; *CWWN*, vol. 22,
   "The Prayer Ministry of the Church," ch. 2

Enlightenment and inspiration: _____

_____

_____

_____

Morning Nourishment

Matt. And do not bring us into temptation, but deliver us
6:13 from the evil one. For Yours is the kingdom and the
power and the glory forever. Amen.
1 Cor. The first man is out of the earth, earthy; the second
15:47 man *is* out of heaven.

As God deals with us, He always cares for three of His divine
attributes—His righteousness, holiness, and glory. God is righteous, God is holy, and God is a God of glory. Righteousness is
related to God's acts, to His ways, actions, and activities. Everything God does is righteous. Holiness is God's nature. Holiness is
not a matter of action, but of nature. As the nature of a table
is wood and the nature of a book is paper, so the nature of God is
holiness. God's acts are righteous and His nature is holiness....
Glory is God Himself expressed. When God is expressed, that is
glory. Therefore, in righteousness we see God's ways, in holiness
we see God's nature, and in glory we see God expressed. (*Life-
study of Romans*, p. 203)

Today's Reading

[In Matthew 6:13] is the realization and praise of God's
kingdom, power, and glory. This also refers to the Triune God.
The kingdom is of the Son, which is the realm in which God exercises His power. The power is of the Spirit, which carries out
God's intention so that the Father can express His glory. This
indicates that the prayer which the Lord teaches us to pray
begins with the Triune God, in the sequence of the Father, the
Son, and the Spirit, and ends also with the Triune God, but in
the sequence of the Son, the Spirit, and the Father. Thus, the
prayer taught by the Lord in His supreme teaching begins with
God the Father and ends also with God the Father. God the
Father is both the beginning and the end, the Alpha and the
Omega. (*The God-man Living*, p. 100)

Has this been accomplished? Certainly not. Yet, God created
man with this intention. Satan knows this much better than we
do. The Bible tells us that immediately after the creation of man,

Satan came in to damage the man whom God had created for His purpose. Man fell. However, God did not give man up. God Himself became a man. He came that He might get into man and make Himself one with man. He came to be the second man called Jesus (1 Cor. 15:47). The first man did not fulfill God's purpose; the second man did. The first man was a corporate man, and the second man is also a corporate man. Adam was the head of the first corporate man, and Christ is the Head of the second man. God's purpose is fulfilled by the second man....The fulfillment of God's purpose in giving man dominion started with Christ.

The preaching in the New Testament begins in a peculiar way, in a way that is contrary to our concept. It says, "Repent, for the kingdom of the heavens has drawn near" (Matt. 4:17). The words *has drawn near* mean "is come." When Christ came, the kingdom of God came. Christ brought in the kingdom. The little man Jesus was the kingdom of God.

The fulfillment of God's intention in giving man dominion involves Christ as the Head and the church, including all the saints, as the Body. The fulfillment of God's intention is not only with the Head, but also with the Body. The gates of Hades cannot prevail against the church (Matt. 16:18). The Bible does not say the gates of Hades (meaning the power of Satan) cannot prevail against the saints. They can prevail against the saints if the saints are separate or individualistic. You need to be built into the church. The Body which is built up with Christ can never be defeated by Satan. Satan can never prevail against the builded church.

The saints have been given authority to bind the enemy (Matt. 16:19; 18:18). The word in Matthew 16:19 was spoken to Peter; the word in Matthew 18:18 was spoken to every believer....Today, the church with all the saints has the authority to bind and loose. Many times, we should not simply pray; we should bind and loose. (*Life-study of Genesis,* pp. 83-84, 86)

Further Reading: Life-study of Genesis, msgs. 7-8; *The Experience of Life,* chs. 17-18

Enlightenment and inspiration: _____

_____

_____

_____

Morning Nourishment

Rom.
5:19

For just as through the disobedience of one man the many were constituted sinners, so also through the obedience of the One the many will be constituted righteous.

Eph.
2:15

Abolishing in His flesh the law of the command-ments in ordinances, that He might create the two in Himself into one new man, *so* making peace.

First Corinthians 15:47 says, "The first man is out of the earth, earthy; the second man is out of heaven." Christ is not only the last Adam but also the second man. The first Adam is the beginning of the old man in the old creation; the last Adam is the ending, the termination of the old man in the old creation.

As the first man, Adam is the head of the old creation, repre-senting it in creation. As the second man, Christ is Head of the new creation, representing it in resurrection. In the entire uni-verse there are these two men: the first man Adam, including all his descendants, and the second man Christ, comprised of all His believers. We believers were included in the first man by birth, and we became a part of the second man by regenera-tion. Our belief has transferred us out of the first man into the second. As a part of the first man, our origin is the earth, and our nature is earthy. As a part of the second man, our origin is God, and our nature is heavenly. (*The Divine Dispensing of the Divine Trinity*, p. 72)

Today's Reading

We must go on to see the crucial importance of Christ's abol-ishing the law of the commandments in ordinances in order to create us into one new man.

The fact that the Jews and the Gentiles have been created into one new man indicates that the new man is an entity that is corporate and universal. There are many believers, but there is just one new man. All the believers are part of this one corporate and universal new man. The highest revelation of the church given in the book of Ephesians is that of the new man.

To be regenerated is not only to be saved; it is also to be created anew. On the cross Christ abolished the ordinances so that a re-creation could take place. The Jews and the Gentiles were separated by ordinances. But the two peoples have been created in Christ with the divine essence into one new entity, the corporate new man.

In order to see the one new man, we need to have a proper understanding of the old man. Before exhorting us to put on the new man, Paul tells us to put off the old man (Eph. 4:22). After creating heaven and earth, God created man, not merely as an individual, but as a collective entity. Genesis 1:26 speaks of man both in the singular and in the plural: "And God said, Let Us make man in Our image, according to Our likeness; and let them have dominion...." This reveals that God's intention has always been to have one collective man. The corporate man created by God was damaged through the fall, and there is now the need for God to have a new man. In order to produce this new man, Christ had to deal not only with sin, the fallen nature of the old man, Satan, and the world, but as we have pointed out, He also had to abolish the ordinances. What most frustrates God from gaining the new man is ordinances. When Christ was crucified on the cross, our sins, our old man, Satan, and the world were not the only things crucified; all the ordinances were crucified also. The crucifixion of the ordinances was not for forgiveness, holiness, victory over Satan, or the imparting of life; rather, it was absolutely for the creation of the one new man.

We are familiar with such verses as John 1:1 and 3:16, but we are not familiar with Ephesians 2:15....When Christ's flesh was nailed to the cross, He abolished the law of the commandments in ordinances so that He might create the two, the Jews and Gentiles, in Himself into one new man. (*Life-study of Ephesians*, pp. 654, 207-208)

Further Reading: The One New Man, chs. 3-5; *Life-study of Ephesians*, msgs. 23-25

Enlightenment and inspiration: _____

_____

_____

_____

Morning Nourishment

Eph. **And put on the new man, which was created ac-**
4:24 **cording to God in righteousness and holiness of**
the reality.

Rev. **And night will be no more; and they have no need**
22:5 **of the light of a lamp and of the light of the sun, for**
the Lord God will shine upon them; and they will
reign forever and ever.

God's creation of man in Genesis 1 is a picture of the new man
in God's new creation. This means that the old creation is a figure,
a type, of the new creation. In God's old creation the central char-
acter is man. It is the same in God's new creation. Therefore, in
both the old creation and the new creation man is the center.

God created man in His own image (Gen. 1:26) and then gave
man His dominion. Image is for expression. God wants man to
be His expression. Dominion, however, is a matter not of expression but of representation. God wants man to represent Him in
His authority for His dominion.

The image refers to God's positive intention, and dominion to
God's negative intention. God's positive intention is that man
would express Him, whereas God's negative intention is that
man would deal with God's enemy, Satan, the devil. (*The Conclusion of the New Testament*, p. 2302)

Today's Reading

In the old creation the dominion given to man was limited to
the earth. This means that in the old creation the dealing with
God's enemy was restricted to the earth. However, in God's new
creation the dominion has been enlarged to the entire universe.

Eventually, the church as the new man is the man in God's
intention. God wanted a man, and in the old creation He created a figure, a type, not the real man. The real man is the man
Christ created on the cross through His all-inclusive death.
This man is called the new man.

The term *the new man* reminds us of the old man. The old
man did not fulfill God's dual purpose. However, the new man in

God's new creation does fulfill the twofold purpose of expressing God and dealing with God's enemy. (*The Conclusion of the New Testament,* p. 2303)

According to Genesis 1, God created man in His own image and gave man His authority to rule over all the created things.... Man is in the image of God in order to express God, and he has received God's authority in order to represent God. We need God's authority to represent God and to subdue His enemy.

In order to have the full image of God to express God and to realize the full authority of God to represent God in subduing His enemy, we must have God as life to us. Therefore, in the first two chapters of Genesis, there is not only image and authority but also life, signified by the tree of life. We need to take in the divine life of God for two reasons: positively, so that we can express God; negatively, so that we can represent God to subdue His enemy. The authority of God is a matter of the kingdom. Throughout the entire Scriptures there is a line of authority related to the kingdom. (*CWWL, 1972,* vol. 2, "The Kingdom," p. 3)

In eternity the whole New Jerusalem will express God. Furthermore, in eternity all the saved ones in the New Jerusalem will reign as kings with God (Rev. 22:5). This will be the dominion to represent God.

Although we did not care about God's dominion and image at the time we were called and saved, deep within, in God's calling and speaking, we realized that these matters were implied. After being saved, we had the realization that we needed to be under God's ruling. This is the kingdom, the dominion. Also, deep within us, we had the sensation that, after being saved, we had to glorify God. This is the matter of image to express God....Praise the Lord that in God's recovery He has recovered us to His original purpose, and He has brought us back to the beginning. (*Life-study of Genesis,* p. 537)

Further Reading: CWWL, 1972, vol. 2, pp. 57-63; *The One New Man,* chs. 1-2; *The Conclusion of the New Testament,* msgs. 216-218

Enlightenment and inspiration: _____

_____

_____

_____

Hymns, #892

1   With all the pow'r in heav'n and earth
     Our resurrected Lord's endued;
     If we unite and live by Him,
     The enemy will be subdued.

2   In Jesus' name we must declare
     That we shall overcome the foe;
     We draw authority from Him
     The serpent's head to crush below.

3   No matter what, thou mountain high,
     In heav'n or earth, where'er thou art,
     At any cost we'll level thee,
     In Jesus' name thou must depart!

4   Faith orders thee "Remove from here,
     And be thou cast into the sea!"
     We should, we must, we can, we will,
     Fulfill God's purpose faithfully.

Composition for prophecy with main point and sub-points: _____

_____

_____

_____

_____

_____

_____

_____

_____

_____

_____

_____

_____

_____

_____

_____

_____

_____

_____

_____

_____

_____

_____

_____

_____

_____

_____

_____

_____

_____

_____

_____

_____

_____

The Tree of Life
and the Tree of the Knowledge
of Good and Evil

Scripture Reading: Gen. 2:9, 16-17; John 5:39-40; 2 Cor. 3:6b

Day 1
I. **The tree of life signifies Christ, who imparts life to man and who pleases and satisfies man (Gen. 2:9; John 14:6a; 10:10b; 6:63; 1 Cor. 15:45b; cf. John 15:1; Exo. 15:25):**
   A. The tree of life is the center of the universe; according to the purpose of God, the earth is the center of the universe, the garden of Eden is the center of the earth, and the tree of life is the center of the garden of Eden.
   B. We must realize that the whole universe is centered on this tree of life; nothing is more central and crucial to both God and man than this tree.
   C. God's placing man in front of the tree of life indicates that God wanted man to receive Him as man's life by eating Him organically and assimilating Him metabolically so that God might become the very constituent of man's being (John 6:35, 57).
   D. According to John 1:1 and 4, life is in the Word, who is God Himself; this life—the divine, eternal, uncreated life of God—is Christ (11:25; 14:6a; Col. 3:4a), who is the embodiment of God (2:9).
   E. The tree of life grows along the two sides of the river of water of life (Rev. 22:1-2), indicating that it is a vine; since Christ is a vine tree (John 15:1) and is also life, He is the tree of life.
   F. Christ was processed through incarnation, crucifixion, and resurrection so that man may have life and live by eating Him (10:10b; 6:51, 57, 63).

Day 2
II. **The tree of the knowledge of good and evil signifies Satan as the source of death to man (Gen. 2:9, 17; Heb. 2:14):**

A. The tree of the knowledge of good and evil also signifies all things apart from God, for anything that is not God Himself, including good things and even scriptural things and religious things, can be utilized by Satan, the subtle one, to bring death to man.

B. Even the Scriptures inspired by God and the law given by God can be utilized by Satan as the tree of knowledge to bring in death (John 5:39-40; 2 Cor. 3:6).

Day 3 III. **God's first commandment to man concerned man's eating, not man's conduct (Gen. 2:16-17):**

A. Eating is critical to man, a matter of life or death; man's outcome and destiny before God depend altogether on what he eats.

B. If man eats the tree of life, he will receive God as life and fulfill God's purpose; if he eats the tree of knowledge, he will receive Satan as death and be usurped by him for his purpose.

C. God's forbidding commandment, given as a warning to man (vv. 16-17; cf. Eph. 2:1), indicates the following:

1. It indicates God's greatness in creating man with a free will so that man may choose God willingly and not under coercion.

2. It indicates God's love for man.

3. It indicates God's desire that man would eat the tree of life to receive God into him as his life.

Day 4 IV. **The tree of life causes man to be dependent on God (John 15:5), whereas the tree of knowledge causes man to rebel against God and to be independent from Him (cf. Gen. 3:5):**

A. The two trees issue in two lines—the line of life and the line of death—that run through the entire Bible and end in the book of Revelation.

B. Death begins with the tree of knowledge (Gen. 2:17) and ends with the lake of fire (Rev. 20:10, 14); life begins with the tree of life and ends in the New Jerusalem, the city of the water of life (22:1-2).

Day 5 V. **We need to see the line of the tree of life throughout the Scriptures:**
A. Abel contacted God in God's way (Gen. 4:4).
B. Seth and Enosh called upon the name of the Lord (v. 26).
C. Enoch walked with God (5:22, 24).
D. Noah walked with God and worked together with God (6:9, 13-14).
E. Abraham lived in the appearing of God and called upon the name of the Lord (Acts 7:2; Gen. 12:7-8; 17:1; 18:1).
F. Isaac lived in the appearing of God and called upon the name of the Lord (26:2, 24-25).
G. Jacob lived in the appearing of God and called upon the name of the Lord (35:1, 9; 48:3).
Day 6 H. Moses lived in the appearing and the presence of God (Acts 7:30; Exo. 3:2, 16; 33:11, 13-15; 34:29; 25:9).
I. The children of Israel journeyed in the presence of the Lord (13:21-22; Num. 14:14).
J. Joshua lived and worked in the presence of the Lord (Josh. 1:5-9).
K. Gideon fought the battle in the presence of the Lord (Judg. 6:12, 16).
L. Samuel prayed and called upon the name of the Lord (1 Sam. 12:23; 15:11; Psa. 99:6; Jer. 15:1).
M. David trusted in God, looked to God, and enjoyed God as life (1 Sam. 17:37, 45; 30:6; Psa. 27:4, 8, 14; 36:8-9).
N. Daniel prayed to God constantly and contacted Him continually (Dan. 6:10-11; 9:2-4; 10:1-3, 12).
O. Jesus as the Son of God lived by God (John 5:19; 6:57; 14:10).
P. The New Testament believers live by the Lord and enjoy the Lord (15:5; 6:57; 14:19; 6:35; 15:11; 16:24; 17:13; 1 John 1:4).
Q. Paul lived out the Lord (Gal. 2:20; Phil. 1:19-21a).
R. The church as the Body of Christ lives by Christ as life (Eph. 1:22-23; Col. 3:4).

S. The New Jerusalem is sustained by the river of water of life with the tree of life (Rev. 22:1-2).

VI. **We need to see the line of the tree of knowledge throughout the Scriptures:**

A. Cain presented an offering to God in his own way, not in God's way; he murdered his brother and went out from the presence of the Lord (Gen. 4:3-9, 16).

B. Nimrod, a mighty hunter before the Lord, was a person who was absolutely independent of God, building a kingdom for himself, and the beginning of his kingdom was Babel (10:8-11).

C. The people at Babel held a council, and the result was the construction of a high tower for man's name and the formation of a city for his possession (11:3-4).

D. Lot drifted away from the line of life by making a choice according to his own sight (13:10-13, cf. vv. 14-15, 18).

E. Esau, for the purpose of satisfying his appetite, sold his birthright (25:30-34).

F. Pharaoh was rebellious against God, and his heart was hardened toward God (Exo. 5:2; 7:13, 22; 8:15, 19, 32; 9:34-35).

G. Aaron listened to the people and acted independently to make a golden idol (32:1, 4, 24).

H. Nadab and Abihu offered "strange fire" to God (Lev. 10:1-2).

I. Miriam and Aaron were opposed to Moses, not as a result of their contacting God but because of their own motive (Num. 12:1-2, 9-15).

J. The ten spies failed because they looked at the situation in the land by their own sight; they failed because they relied on their knowledge and refused to trust in the Lord (13:28, 32-33, cf. v. 30; 14:6-9).

K. Korah and his company attacked God's deputy authority (16:1-3).

L. Saul acted independently and did not follow the

Lord; rather, he dealt with the enemy according to his preference (1 Sam. 15:8, 11, 22-23).

M. Absalom rebelled against his father, King David (2 Sam. 15:10-13).

N. Ahab was an evil king who married Jezebel, a devilish and idolatrous woman, and built a temple for Baal, the most famous idol of the time (1 King 16:30-32).

O. The chief priests and the scribes knew the letter of the Bible but not the life of the Bible (Matt. 2:4-6).

P. Nicodemus was seeking knowledge, but what he needed was a new life (John 3:1-3).

Q. The Jewish religionists searched the Scriptures thinking that in them they had eternal life, yet they would not come to the Lord for that very life (5:39-40).

R. The scribes and Pharisees held the knowledge of the law but were still under the slavery of sin (8:5, 9, 34).

S. The disciples who were with the Lord still held the traditional knowledge of religion when they saw a man blind from birth (9:1-3).

T. Martha was occupied with the line of knowledge, holding the knowledge of the sound teachings regarding the resurrection in the last day (11:23-25).

U. Peter, after receiving the revelation from the heavenly Father, turned to his mind and was utilized by Satan to frustrate the Lord from going to the cross (Matt. 16:17, 21-23).

V. Judas, who was always occupied with thoughts of money, opened himself to the devil and betrayed the Lord for thirty pieces of silver (John 12:4-6; 13:2, 27; Matt. 26:15; 27:5).

W. The unbelieving Jews kept their law and sentenced the Lord Jesus to death according to it (John 19:7).

X. Saul of Tarsus, a foremost religionist, persecuted

the church until God revealed His Son in him
(Gal. 1:13-16; 2:20).

Y. The Corinthian believers were enriched in all
knowledge but were puffed up and still infants
in Christ (1 Cor. 1:5; 8:1; 3:1).

Z. The Gnostic philosophy distracted and spoiled
many believers from enjoying Christ as their
life (Col. 2:8, cf. v. 6).

AA. The dissenters in the church make divisions
and causes of stumbling contrary to the teaching of God's economy (Rom. 16:17; 1 Tim. 1:4).

BB. The teaching of Balaam, the teaching of the Nico-
laitans, and the teaching of Jezebel deceived the
early churches, who turned away from the eating of and feasting with the Lord (Rev. 2:14-15,
20, 24, 7, 17; 3:20).

CC. Antichrist will be the man of lawlessness, the
son of perdition; he will be the giant on the line
of knowledge, and his destiny is to be cast into
the lake of fire with Satan, the source of death
(13:5-8; 2 Thes. 2:3-4; Rev. 19:20; 20:10).

DD. "The letter kills, but the Spirit gives life" (2 Cor.
3:6b):

1. The Bible in dead letters, which belongs to
the tree of knowledge, kills, but the Spirit,
who belongs to the tree of life, gives life.

2. Besides the line of knowledge there is the
line of life (cf. Deut. 30:19-20); praise the
Lord for the choice of life!

Morning Nourishment

Gen. **And out of the ground Jehovah God caused to**
2:9 **grow every tree that is pleasant to the sight and**
good for food, as well as the tree of life in the
middle of the garden and the tree of the knowledge
of good and evil.
John **I am the true vine, and My Father is the husband-**
15:1 **man.**
6:48 **I am the bread of life.**

The second step of God's procedure in fulfilling His purpose was to place the created man in front of the tree of life, which signifies the Triune God embodied in Christ as life to man in the form of food. God's placing man in front of the tree of life indicates that God wanted man to receive Him as man's life by eating Him organically and assimilating Him metabolically, that God might become the very constituent of man's being. According to John 1:1, 4, life is in the Word, who is God Himself. This life—the divine, eternal, uncreated life of God—is Christ (John 11:25; 14:6; Col. 3:4a), who is the embodiment of God (Col. 2:9). The tree of life grows along the two sides of the river of water of life (Rev. 22:1-2), indicating that it is a vine. Since Christ is a vine tree (John 15:1) and is also life, He is the tree of life. He was processed through incarnation, crucifixion, and resurrection that man might have life and live by eating Him (John 10:10b; 6:51, 57, 63). (Gen. 2:9, footnote 2)

Today's Reading

The tree of life was in the midst of the garden. If we study the record of Genesis 2, we will realize that, apart from the tree of knowledge of good and evil, no tree is mentioned by name except the tree of life. We do not know the names of the other trees, but we do know that there was a tree called the tree of life. This shows that the tree of life was the center.

The tree of life is the center of the universe. According to the purpose of God, the earth is the center of the universe, the garden of Eden is the center of the earth, and the tree of life is the center of the garden of Eden. We must realize that the whole universe is centered on this tree of life: nothing is more central and crucial to both God and man than this tree. It is very meaningful to see man in the garden standing before the tree of life.

This tree enables man to receive God as life. How can we prove this? The following books of the Bible reveal that God is life. Therefore, the tree of life in the garden was the indicator that God intends to be our life in the form of food. One day, according to the Gospel of John, God came in the flesh (John 1:1, 14). In Him was life (John 1:4). The life displayed by the tree of life in Genesis 2 was the life incarnated in Jesus, God in the flesh. Jesus told us that He Himself is life (John 14:6). Furthermore, John 15 tells us that Christ is a tree, the vine tree. On the one hand, He is a tree; on the other hand, He is life. When we put together all these portions from John, we see that Jesus is the tree of life. Jesus said that He is the bread of life, meaning that He has come to us as the tree of life in the form of food.

As the almighty God, Jesus is high, but when He came to us as food He was lowly. He was a loaf of bread. He was even the crumbs under the table (Matt. 15:21-27). The very Jesus who came to us as life in the form of food was not tall and great; He was small and lowly. Anything we eat must be smaller than we are; if it is not, we cannot take it into us. Even if our food is larger than we are, it must be cut into pieces small enough to eat. Thus, Jesus came to us as life in the form of food. He said, "I am the bread of life," and, "He who eats Me, he also shall live because of Me" [John 6:48, 57]. God in the Son is the tree of life that is good for food. Day after day we can feed on Him. We can eat Him.

The tree of life typifies Christ who imparts life to man and who pleases and satisfies man (cf. John 15:1; Exo. 15:25). Christ imparts divine life into us, pleases us, and satisfies us. Many of us can testify of this. We can say, "Hallelujah! Jesus has imparted life to me. He satisfies me all the time." This is the tree of life. (*Life-study of Genesis,* pp. 140-141)

Further Reading: Life-study of Genesis, msg. 11

Enlightenment and inspiration: _____

_____

_____

_____

Morning Nourishment

Gen. But of the tree of the knowledge of good and evil, of
2:17 it you shall not eat; for in the day that you eat of it
you shall surely die.

2 Cor. Who has also made us sufficient as ministers of a
3:6 new covenant, *ministers* not of the letter but of the
Spirit; for the letter kills, but the Spirit gives life.

The tree of life was a symbol, signifying God as the proper
source....If we only read Genesis 2, we will be unable to understand the meaning of the tree of life. However, the Gospel of
John reveals the life denoted by the tree of life in a concrete
way. John 1:4 says, "In Him was life," and John 15:5 tells us
that the Lord Jesus is a vine tree. If we put these two verses
together, we will realize that Christ is the tree of life. Jesus, the
embodiment of God, is the tree of life. Therefore, the tree of life
in Genesis 2 is a symbol of God as the source of life.

Besides this source, there is another tree, another source in
the universe—death. However, this tree is not called the tree of
death; it is called the tree of the knowledge of good and evil.
There is such a tree in this universe. These two trees oppose one
another, the tree of life denoting God as the source of life, and the
tree of knowledge signifying Satan as the source of death....
Therefore, in Genesis 2 we find two sources signified by two
trees. (*Life-study of Genesis,* pp. 161-162)

Today's Reading

The principle of the tree of life...is dependence. We all must
be dependent. Do not take the way of knowledge, for the result
of that way is death.

The tree of knowledge (Gen. 2:17), which was the opposite of
the tree of life,...was called the tree of knowledge of good and
evil, not simply the knowledge of evil. Both the knowledge of
good and the knowledge of evil come from the same tree. It does
not matter whether knowledge is the knowledge of good or of
evil. As long as it is knowledge, it does not belong to the tree
of life. It belongs to the tree of knowledge.

Although the tree of the knowledge of good and evil signifies Satan, it does not signify him directly. It firstly signifies everything apart from God and then it signifies Satan indirectly, because Satan is hidden at the back of the things that are apart from God. Satan likes to conceal himself.

God is very frank and always comes to the front. Satan, however, is subtle, always staying at the rear....Because Satan is subtle, the tree of knowledge does not signify him directly. It signifies everything apart from God, including good things, scriptural things, and religious things. Regardless of whether a thing is good or evil, as long as it is not God Himself it can be utilized by Satan.

The things apart from God fall into three categories: knowledge, good, and evil. Suppose you have the intention of doing a certain good thing. Deep in your spirit, however, you have the sense not to touch it and not to do it....Do not employ the principle of good and bad, but cooperate with the principle of life. If you do not have peace within, it means that the Spirit of life does not agree with what you intend to do. You need to cooperate with Him. If you do, you will receive life.

The tree of knowledge firstly signifies everything utilized by Satan, regardless of whether it is good or evil. It does not signify Satan directly, because he likes to hide. When Satan first entered into man, he did not do it in a frank way. He came in the form of a serpent. At the beginning of the Bible, the serpent was very cunning and apparently was quite attractive (Gen. 3:1), unlike the ugly serpents under God's curse. As Eve conversed with the serpent, she did not realize that Satan was in it. Herein lies the principle of Satan's appearing: he never appears frankly, but subtly.

The contents of the tree of knowledge are all things apart from God. Even the Bible inspired by God and the law given by God may be utilized in letters by Satan as the tree of knowledge. (*Life-study of Genesis,* pp. 165-167)

Further Reading: Life-study of Genesis, msg. 13

Enlightenment and inspiration: _____

_____

_____

_____

Morning Nourishment

Gen. And Jehovah God commanded the man, saying, Of
2:16-17 every tree of the garden you may eat freely, but
of the tree of the knowledge of good and evil, of
it you shall not eat; for in the day that you eat of it
you shall surely die.
Eph. And you, though dead in your offenses and sins.
2:1

God's first commandment to man concerned man's eating, not
man's conduct. Eating is critical to man, a matter of life or death.
Man's outcome and destiny before God depends altogether on
what he eats. If man eats the tree of life, he will receive God as life
and fulfill God's purpose; if he eats the tree of knowledge, he will
receive Satan as death and be usurped by him for his purpose.

God's forbidding commandment given as a warning to man
indicates (1) God's greatness in creating man with a free will
that man may choose God willingly and not under coercion; (2)
God's love for man; and (3) God's desire that man would eat the
tree of life to receive God into him as life. (Gen. 2:17, footnote 1)

Today's Reading

Genesis 2:17 tells us that God issued man a warning and
gave him a prohibition. God wanted man only to touch Him to
receive life, but not to touch the things apart from God to receive
death. God seemed to tell Adam and Eve, "Don't touch the tree of
knowledge—only touch the tree of life. If you eat the tree of life,
you will receive Me and have My life. If you eat the tree of knowledge, you will take in Satan and have his death." This was not
merely a commandment; it was a warning. We must realize that
in the whole universe there are two sources: one is the source of
life, and the other is the source of death. Be careful which source
you touch. If you touch God, you have the source of life and
receive life. If you touch Satan, you have the source of death
and receive death. (*Life-study of Genesis,* p. 179)

Genesis tells us that after God created man, He put man in
front of the tree of life. God did not give man a list of commandments. That was the work of Moses after the fall, not the

work of God according to His eternal intention. The] Exodus 20, not in Genesis 2. In Genesis 2 is the first picture regarding God's dealing with His created man. There is such a basic principle of the first mentioning in the Bible. Whenever you have the first mentioning, a principle is always laid. The first mentioning of God's dealing with man is that God put Adam in front of the tree of life, charging him to be careful about his eating (vv. 16-17). God's intention for man is not a matter of doing but a matter of eating. If man eats well and eats rightly, then he will be right.

This tree of life is God in Christ as the Spirit to be life to us. It is the Triune God, the Father in the Son, and the Son as the Spirit. Before we received the Lord, we may not have thought anything about God. But when we got saved or revived, we might have immediately made up our mind to serve the Lord, to do our best to do good deeds to please Him, and to "go to church" to worship Him. These thoughts, which are according to our natural concept, are wrong. God's intention is not that we serve Him, do good to please Him, or that we worship Him in a religious, ritualistic way. But God's intention is that we eat Him. We have to eat Him. The first picture of God's dealing with man is not a picture of doing but a picture of eating.

We all have to first realize that the Lord has no intention that we do something for Him. The Lord's intention is to present Himself as food to us day by day. In the Gospel of John the Lord is first seen as life (1:4), as the bread of life (6:35), as the water of life (4:14), and as the breath of life, the air (20:22). He is life, food, drink, and air. All this is not for you to be a doing Christian but to be an enjoying Christian. You have to enjoy the Lord as life, as food, as water, and as air. You have to breathe Him in, to drink of Him, and to feed on Him in order to live by Him and in Him. (*CWWL, 1965,* vol. 2, "The Tree of Life," pp. 83, 85)

Further Reading: Life-study of Genesis, msg. 14; *CWWL, 1965,* vol. 2, "The Tree of Life," ch. 1

Enlightenment and inspiration: Lord, Help me to eat, drink, breathe and live by your word day by day. To be fully constituted with you in Jesus' name. Amen

Morning Nourishment

John I am the vine; you are the branches. He who abides
15:5 in Me and I in him, he bears much fruit; for apart
from Me you can do nothing.

Gen. For God knows that in the day you eat of it your
3:5 eyes will be opened, and you will become like God,
knowing good and evil.

The tree of the knowledge of good and evil signifies Satan as
the source of death to man (Heb. 2:14). It also signifies all things
apart from God....Even the Scriptures inspired by God and the
law given by God can be utilized by Satan as the tree of knowledge to bring in death (John 5:39-40; 2 Cor. 3:6b).

The tree of life causes man to be dependent on God (John
15:5), whereas the tree of knowledge causes man to rebel
against God and to be independent from Him (cf. Gen. 3:5). The
two trees issue in two lines—the line of life and the line of
death—that run through the entire Bible and end in the book
of Revelation. Death begins with the tree of knowledge (Gen. 2:17)
and ends with the lake of fire (Rev. 20:10, 14). Life begins with
the tree of life and ends in the New Jerusalem, the city of the
water of life (22:1-2). (Gen. 2:9, footnote 3)

Today's Reading

The record of the two trees in Genesis 2, the tree of life and
the tree of knowledge, is not merely ancient history, for these two
trees are still with us today. If we read the Bible carefully, we
will discover that throughout the Bible we have two lines—the
line of the tree of life and the line of the tree of knowledge. We
may refer to them in brief as the line of life and the line of knowledge. These two lines began at the book of Genesis and continue
through the subsequent books of the Bible until they reach their
destination....The destination of the line of life will be the New
Jerusalem, where the tree of life appears once again. The river of
the water of life is also found in the New Jerusalem, for it flows
throughout the entire city. Thus, the New Jerusalem, a city of
living water, is the ultimate consummation of the line of the tree

of life. The line of knowledge will conclude with the lake of fire, a
vivid contrast to the city of New Jerusalem. The city is a city of
living water; the lake is a lake of burning fire.

According to the revelation in the Bible, we see two streams
proceeding out of the throne of God. One is the stream of living
water, and the other is a stream of fire. The stream of living water
is revealed in Ezekiel 47 and Revelation 22. In Ezekiel living water issues out of the house of God; in Revelation 22 living water
flows out of the throne of God. In Daniel 7:9-10 we see another
stream, a stream of fire, flowing out of the throne of God. The living water is for reviving and watering, but the stream of fire is
for judging. It courses in judgment throughout the universe. The
river of water proceeds out of the throne of God and will flow all
positive things into the New Jerusalem. The stream of fire issues
out of the throne of God and will sweep all negative things into the
lake of fire. In the beginning of the Bible we have the start of two
lines, the line of life and the line of knowledge. At the end of the
Bible we have two results, two consummations—the city of living
water and the lake of burning fire.

Where are you and where are you going? Which line are you
on?... As redeemed people we are surely on the right line, the line
of life. However, it is possible that our walk and our work—that is,
the way we live and work for God—might be on the wrong line....
The Bible firstly warns people to stay away from the line of
knowledge and remain on or return to the line of life. Once we
are saved, we are eternally saved, and our salvation is eternally
secure. Nevertheless, the Bible warns us concerning our daily
walk and our work for the Lord. In Galatians Paul warns us to
walk in the Spirit (5:16) and to sow to the Spirit (6:7-8)....If we
build the church with gold, silver, and precious stones, this work
will continue unto the New Jerusalem....On the other hand, Paul
warns us that the wood, grass, and straw are only useful for burning (1 Cor. 3:12-15). (*Life-study of Genesis,* pp. 181-183)

Further Reading: Life-study of Genesis, msg. 15

Enlightenment and inspiration: _____

_____
_____
_____

Lord; You are My Way

Morning Nourishment

Gen. **And Abel also brought** *an offering,* **from the first-**
4:4 **lings of his flock, that is, from their fat portions. And**
Jehovah had regard for Abel and for his offering.
5:24 **And Enoch walked with God, and he was not, for**
God took him.

Apparently the tree of life has been closed to man; actually through the promised redemption it has been available through-out the ages for God's people to touch, enjoy, and experience. Now in a very simple way I want to give you many of the positive per-sons on this line of life....We begin with Abel.

The characteristic of Abel's life was that he contacted God in God's way (Gen. 4:4). Do not say that as long as you contact God ev-erything is all right. In whose way do you contact God—in your way or God's?...We should observe the example of Abel and contact God by laying aside our thought, opinion, and concept. "Lord, I contact You in Your way. I don't contact You by my thought, concept, or knowledge. Lord, You are my way." If we do this, we will enjoy God as the tree of life. Abel did partake of God as the tree of life. He truly ate of the fruit of this tree. (*Life-study of Genesis,* pp. 183-184)

Today's Reading

After Abel was slain, the line of life seemed to be terminated. Nevertheless, Seth and Enosh were raised up to continue it. These two generations had one outstanding characteristic—they began to call upon the name of the Lord (Gen. 4:26). They not only prayed, but called on the name of the Lord. If you read the original text of the Hebrew and Greek, you will see that the word call means to cry out, not only to pray....To call on the name of the Lord is simply to enjoy Him and to eat Him as the tree of life.

The characteristic of Enoch's life was that he walked with God (Gen. 5:22, 24). We are not told that he worked for God or that he did great things for God, but that he walked with God. This is very meaningful. In order to walk with a person, you must like him. If I do not like you, I will never walk with you. Firstly, I like you, then I love you, and then I will walk with you continually. The fact that

Enoch walked with God.

Enoch walked with God proves that he loved God. He simply loved to be in the presence of God....He was raptured on the basis of his walk with God for a period of three hundred years. Enoch offered us an excellent example.

Noah followed Enoch's footsteps and also walked with God (Gen. 6:9). Actually, he walked with God for a period even longer than three hundred years. As Noah walked with God, God showed him a vision of what He wanted to do in that age. Noah received the vision of the ark used to save eight members of the fallen race. Like Noah, we should not act according to our concept. Whatever we do and work should be according to the vision we received in walking with the Lord. In our daily walk with the Lord we will come to see His desire, His mind, and His will. Then we will work and serve according to God's desire, not according to our own thoughts. Noah enjoyed God by walking with Him.

Abraham was transfused with the appearing of the God of glory. While Abraham was in Ur of the Chaldees, the God of glory appeared to him and attracted him (Acts 7:2). According to the record in Genesis, God appeared to Abraham several other times as well (Gen. 12:7; 17:1; 18:1). Abraham was not a giant of faith by himself; he was as weak as we are. The God of glory appeared to Abraham again and again, each time transfusing and infusing His divine elements into him, enabling him to live by the faith of God....Abraham walked according to the appearing of God.

In addition to experiencing the appearings of God, Abraham called upon the name of the Lord (Gen. 12:7-8). Abraham's son, Isaac, and his grandson, Jacob, also called upon the name of the Lord. Since these three generations were all the same, God was called the God of Abraham, Isaac, and Jacob. This means that God is the God of His people who live in His appearing and who call upon His name. As Abraham lived in the appearing of God and called upon the name of the Lord, he enjoyed Him as the tree of life. (*Life-study of Genesis,* pp. 184-187)

Further Reading: Two Principles of Living; The Tree of Life, ch. 2

Enlightenment and inspiration: _____

_____

_____

_____

Morning Nourishment

Exo. And He said, My presence shall *go with you,* and I
33:14 will give you rest.
John As the living Father has sent Me and I live because
6:57 of the Father, so he who eats Me, he also shall live
because of Me.

God appeared to Moses in a vision of a burning bush, a bush
that burned without being consumed (Exo. 3:2, 16). Moses was
surprised and turned aside to see this bush. It was as if God was
saying to Moses, "Moses, you must be like this burning bush. Do
not burn by yourself or act by yourself. You had a good heart, but
you acted in the wrong way."...Moses learned to cease from his
own knowledge, his own way, his own energy, and his own activities. Moses began to live, as his grandfathers had done, in the
presence and the appearing of the Lord. No longer did he act out
of himself. From that time onward, he was one with God. For the
leading of the Israelites on their journey, the Lord told him, "My
presence shall go with you, and I will give you rest." And he said
to the Lord, "If Your presence does not go with us, do not bring us
up from here" (Exo. 33:13-15). This shows that Moses knew the
necessity of the Lord's presence for his work for the Lord. He was
acting in the presence of God. (*Life-study of Genesis,* pp. 189-190)

Today's Reading

After Moses had brought the children of Israel out of Egypt,
God called him to the mountaintop, where he remained for forty
days. While he was on the mountaintop, he was thoroughly infused
with the shekinah glory of God. As he descended along the side of
the mountain, the glory of God radiated from his face (Exo. 34:29).
On this mountaintop Moses experienced the full enjoyment of God
as the tree of life. Although the tree of life had disappeared from
unbelieving men, it nevertheless appeared to a person like Moses.
Moses enjoyed God as the tree of life on the mount of glory.

David was a man who trusted in God and looked to Him
(1 Sam. 17:37, 45; 30:6). The secret of David's life was that he
desired to dwell continually in the house of God and to behold His

beauty (Psa. 27:4, 8, 14). This means that he enjoyed the presence of God. Moreover, he enjoyed God as the fatness and as the river of joy (Psa. 36:8-9). David said, "With You is the fountain of life." This proves that even in ancient times David enjoyed God's life as the tree of life and as the river flowing within him.

Daniel's prayer life issued out of a holy life. He lived a holy life in the heathen land of Babylon. For example, Daniel refused to eat the king's food, the food which was first offered to idols and then used to feed the king and his people (Dan. 1:8). Daniel refused that food, and he enjoyed God very much. He enjoyed God as the tree of life.

The first person on the line of life in the New Testament was the Lord Jesus. Jesus not only enjoyed the tree of life; He was the tree of life. He Himself said that He came from the Father and that He lived because of the Father (John 6:57). He did not live according to knowledge and learning. He lived, walked, and worked according to the Father who was working within Him (John 14:10).

What should we do today? We should not do anything. We should simply stay on the line of the tree of life, enjoying God as our life and as our life supply. God will take care of everything. Out of the enjoyment of the Lord as our life supply, we will have our daily life, walk, work, and the building up of the churches. Then everything we have will be according to God's divine element, not according to our own concepts....May the Lord have mercy on us that we all may continue on the line of life.

Second Corinthians 3:6...says, "the letter kills, but the Spirit gives life."...The Bible in dead letters, which belongs to the tree of knowledge, kills, while the Spirit, who belongs to the tree of life, gives life. Therefore, we do have a choice. Praise the Lord for this choice! The choice of life! Besides the line of knowledge there is the line of life. We must make a choice between life and knowledge. We must choose between death and life. (*Life-study of Genesis,* pp. 190, 192-195, 211-212)

Further Reading: Life-study of Genesis, msg. 16

Enlightenment and inspiration: _____

_____

_____

_____

Hymns, #1194

1 There are two lines to live by in our living today —
   One the life line to bring us into Christ all the way.
   But the other is knowledge which will make us die;
   We must be very careful on which line we abide.

> Oh, we'll stay on God's life line, never
>   turning aside.
> We don't care for vain knowledge, which
>   will cause us to die.
> Lord, we'll touch You by calling on Your
>   name each day;
> Living in Your appearing, in Your
>   presence we'll stay.

2 Lord, we would be as Abel, fully contacting You;
   Not by knowledge or concept, but by life fresh
      and new.
   Just as Enosh began to call upon Your name,
   And as Enoch who walked with You, we'll do just
      the same.

3 Keep us living and walking as did old Abraham;
   In Your holy appearing to be transfused like him.
   As did Isaac and Jacob, Moses lived this way—
   So dependent upon Your presence with him each day.

4 Full enjoyment had David, ate the life-giving tree.
   Daniel prayed to his God and lived by Him constantly.
   Jesus lived by the Father to be life complete;
   Now as His living Body of the life tree we'll eat.

Composition for prophecy with main point and sub-points: _____

_____

_____

_____

_____

_____

_____

_____

_____

_____

_____

_____

_____

_____

_____

_____

_____

_____

_____

_____

_____

_____

_____

_____

_____

_____

_____

_____

_____

_____

_____

_____

_____

Reading Schedule for the Recovery Version of the Old Testament with Footnotes

Wk.	Lord's Day	Monday	Tuesday	Wednesday	Thursday	Friday	Saturday
1	Gen. 1:1-5 □	1:6-23 □	1:24-31 □	2:1-9 □	2:10-25 □	3:1-13 □	3:14-24 □
2	4:1-26 □	5:1-32 □	6:1-22 □	7:1—8:3 □	8:4-22 □	9:1-29 □	10:1-32 □
3	11:1-32 □	12:1-20 □	13:1-18 □	14:1-24 □	15:1-21 □	16:1-16 □	17:1-27 □
4	18:1-33 □	19:1-38 □	20:1-18 □	21:1-34 □	22:1-24 □	23:1—24:27 □	24:28-67 □
5	25:1-34 □	26:1-35 □	27:1-46 □	28:1-22 □	29:1-35 □	30:1-43 □	31:1-55 □
6	32:1-32 □	33:1—34:31 □	35:1-29 □	36:1-43 □	37:1-36 □	38:1—39:23 □	40:1—41:13 □
7	41:14-57 □	42:1-38 □	43:1-34 □	44:1-34 □	45:1-28 □	46:1-34 □	47:1-31 □
8	48:1-22 □	49:1-15 □	49:16-33 □	50:1-26 □	Exo. 1:1-22 □	2:1-25 □	3:1-22 □
9	4:1-31 □	5:1-23 □	6:1-30 □	7:1-25 □	8:1-32 □	9:1-35 □	10:1-29 □
10	11:1-10 □	12:1-14 □	12:15-36 □	12:37-51 □	13:1-22 □	14:1-31 □	15:1-27 □
11	16:1-36 □	17:1-16 □	18:1-27 □	19:1-25 □	20:1-26 □	21:1-36 □	22:1-31 □
12	23:1-33 □	24:1-18 □	25:1-22 □	25:23-40 □	26:1-14 □	26:15-37 □	27:1-21 □
13	28:1-21 □	28:22-43 □	29:1-21 □	29:22-46 □	30:1-10 □	30:11-38 □	31:1-17 □
14	31:18—32:35 □	33:1-23 □	34:1-35 □	35:1-35 □	36:1-38 □	37:1-29 □	38:1-31 □
15	39:1-43 □	40:1-38 □	Lev. 1:1-17 □	2:1-16 □	3:1-17 □	4:1-35 □	5:1-19 □
16	6:1-30 □	7:1-38 □	8:1-36 □	9:1-24 □	10:1-20 □	11:1-47 □	12:1-8 □
17	13:1-28 □	13:29-59 □	14:1-18 □	14:19-32 □	14:33-57 □	15:1-33 □	16:1-17 □
18	16:18-34 □	17:1-16 □	18:1-30 □	19:1-37 □	20:1-27 □	21:1-24 □	22:1-33 □
19	23:1-22 □	23:23-44 □	24:1-23 □	25:1-23 □	25:24-55 □	26:1-24 □	26:25-46 □
20	27:1-34 □	Num. 1:1-54 □	2:1-34 □	3:1-51 □	4:1-49 □	5:1-31 □	6:1-27 □
21	7:1-41 □	7:42-88 □	7:89—8:26 □	9:1-23 □	10:1-36 □	11:1-35 □	12:1—13:33 □
22	14:1-45 □	15:1-41 □	16:1-50 □	17:1—18:7 □	18:8-32 □	19:1-22 □	20:1-29 □
23	21:1-35 □	22:1-41 □	23:1-30 □	24:1-25 □	25:1-18 □	26:1-65 □	27:1-23 □
24	28:1-31 □	29:1-40 □	30:1—31:24 □	31:25-54 □	32:1-42 □	33:1-56 □	34:1-29 □
25	35:1-34 □	36:1-13 □	Deut. 1:1-46 □	2:1-37 □	3:1-29 □	4:1-49 □	5:1-33 □
26	6:1—7:26 □	8:1-20 □	9:1-29 □	10:1-22 □	11:1-32 □	12:1-32 □	13:1—14:21 □

Reading Schedule for the Recovery Version of the Old Testament with Footnotes

Wk.	Lord's Day	Monday	Tuesday	Wednesday	Thursday	Friday	Saturday
27	14:22—15:23 ☐	16:1-22 ☐	17:1—18:8 ☐	18:9—19:21 ☐	20:1—21:17 ☐	21:18—22:30 ☐	23:1-25 ☐
28	24:1-22 ☐	25:1-19 ☐	26:1-19 ☐	27:1-26 ☐	28:1-68 ☐	29:1-29 ☐	30:1—31:29 ☐
29	31:30—32:52 ☐	33:1-29 ☐	34:1-12 ☐	Josh. 1:1-18 ☐	2:1-24 ☐	3:1-17 ☐	4:1-24 ☐
30	5:1-15 ☐	6:1-27 ☐	7:1-26 ☐	8:1-35 ☐	9:1-27 ☐	10:1-43 ☐	11:1—12:24 ☐
31	13:1-33 ☐	14:1—15:63 ☐	16:1—18:28 ☐	19:1-51 ☐	20:1—21:45 ☐	22:1-34 ☐	23:1—24:33 ☐
32	Judg. 1:1-36 ☐	2:1-23 ☐	3:1-31 ☐	4:1-24 ☐	5:1-31 ☐	6:1-40 ☐	7:1-25 ☐
33	8:1-35 ☐	9:1-57 ☐	10:1—11:40 ☐	12:1—13:25 ☐	14:1—15:20 ☐	16:1-31 ☐	17:1—18:31 ☐
34	19:1-30 ☐	20:1-48 ☐	21:1-25 ☐	Ruth 1:1-22 ☐	2:1-23 ☐	3:1-18 ☐	4:1-22 ☐
35	1 Sam. 1:1-28 ☐	2:1-36 ☐	3:1—4:22 ☐	5:1—6:21 ☐	7:1—8:22 ☐	9:1-27 ☐	10:1—11:15 ☐
36	12:1—13:23 ☐	14:1-52 ☐	15:1-35 ☐	16:1-23 ☐	17:1-58 ☐	18:1-30 ☐	19:1-24 ☐
37	20:1-42 ☐	21:1—22:23 ☐	23:1—24:22 ☐	25:1-44 ☐	26:1-25 ☐	27:1—28:25 ☐	29:1—30:31 ☐
38	31:1-13 ☐	2 Sam. 1:1-27 ☐	2:1-32 ☐	3:1-39 ☐	4:1—5:25 ☐	6:1-23 ☐	7:1-29 ☐
39	8:1—9:13 ☐	10:1—11:27 ☐	12:1-31 ☐	13:1-39 ☐	14:1-33 ☐	15:1—16:23 ☐	17:1—18:33 ☐
40	19:1-43 ☐	20:1—21:22 ☐	22:1-51 ☐	23:1-39 ☐	24:1-25 ☐	1 Kings 1:1-19 ☐	1:20-53 ☐
41	2:1-46 ☐	3:1-28 ☐	4:1-34 ☐	5:1—6:38 ☐	7:1-22 ☐	7:23-51 ☐	8:1-36 ☐
42	8:37-66 ☐	9:1-28 ☐	10:1-29 ☐	11:1-43 ☐	12:1-33 ☐	13:1-34 ☐	14:1-31 ☐
43	15:1-34 ☐	16:1—17:24 ☐	18:1-46 ☐	19:1-21 ☐	20:1-43 ☐	21:1—22:53 ☐	2 Kings 1:1-18 ☐
44	2:1—3:27 ☐	4:1-44 ☐	5:1—6:33 ☐	7:1-20 ☐	8:1-29 ☐	9:1-37 ☐	10:1-36 ☐
45	11:1—12:21 ☐	13:1—14:29 ☐	15:1-38 ☐	16:1-20 ☐	17:1-41 ☐	18:1-37 ☐	19:1-37 ☐
46	20:1—21:26 ☐	22:1-20 ☐	23:1-37 ☐	24:1—25:30 ☐	1 Chron. 1:1-54 ☐	2:1—3:24 ☐	4:1—5:26 ☐
47	6:1-81 ☐	7:1-40 ☐	8:1-40 ☐	9:1-44 ☐	10:1—11:47 ☐	12:1-40 ☐	13:1—14:17 ☐
48	15:1—16:43 ☐	17:1-27 ☐	18:1—19:19 ☐	20:1—21:30 ☐	22:1—23:32 ☐	24:1—25:31 ☐	26:1-32 ☐
49	27:1-34 ☐	28:1—29:30 ☐	2 Chron. 1:1-17 ☐	2:1—3:17 ☐	4:1—5:14 ☐	6:1-42 ☐	7:1—8:18 ☐
50	9:1—10:19 ☐	11:1—12:16 ☐	13:1—15:19 ☐	16:1—17:19 ☐	18:1—19:11 ☐	20:1-37 ☐	21:1—22:12 ☐
51	23:1—24:27 ☐	25:1—26:23 ☐	27:1—28:27 ☐	29:1-36 ☐	30:1—31:21 ☐	32:1-33 ☐	33:1—34:33 ☐
52	35:1—36:23 ☐	Ezra 1:1-11 ☐	2:1-70 ☐	3:1—4:24 ☐	5:1—6:22 ☐	7:1-28 ☐	8:1-36 ☐

Reading Schedule for the Recovery Version of the Old Testament with Footnotes

Wk.	Lord's Day	Monday	Tuesday	Wednesday	Thursday	Friday	Saturday
53	9:1—10:44 ☐	Neh. 1:1-11 ☐	2:1—3:32 ☐	4:1—5:19 ☐	6:1-19 ☐	7:1-73 ☐	8:1-18 ☐
54	9:1-20 ☐	9:21-38 ☐	10:1—11:36 ☐	12:1-47 ☐	13:1-31 ☐	Esth. 1:1-22 ☐	2:1—3:15 ☐
55	4:1—5:14 ☐	6:1—7:10 ☐	8:1-17 ☐	9:1—10:3 ☐	Job 1:1-22 ☐	2:1—3:26 ☐	4:1—5:27 ☐
56	6:1—7:21 ☐	8:1—9:35 ☐	10:1—11:20 ☐	12:1—13:28 ☐	14:1—15:35 ☐	16:1—17:16 ☐	18:1—19:29 ☐
57	20:1—21:34 ☐	22:1—23:17 ☐	24:1—25:6 ☐	26:1—27:23 ☐	28:1—29:25 ☐	30:1—31:40 ☐	32:1—33:33 ☐
58	34:1—35:16 ☐	36:1-33 ☐	37:1-24 ☐	38:1-41 ☐	39:1-30 ☐	40:1-24 ☐	41:1-34 ☐
59	42:1-17 ☐	Psa. 1:1-6 ☐	2:1—3:8 ☐	4:1—6:10 ☐	7:1—8:9 ☐	9:1—10:18 ☐	11:1—15:5 ☐
60	16:1—17:15 ☐	18:1-50 ☐	19:1—21:13 ☐	22:1-31 ☐	23:1—24:10 ☐	25:1—27:14 ☐	28:1—30:12 ☐
61	31:1—32:11 ☐	33:1—34:22 ☐	35:1—36:12 ☐	37:1-40 ☐	38:1—39:13 ☐	40:1—41:13 ☐	42:1—43:5 ☐
62	44:1-26 ☐	45:1-17 ☐	46:1—48:14 ☐	49:1—50:23 ☐	51:1—52:9 ☐	53:1—55:23 ☐	56:1—58:11 ☐
63	59:1—61:8 ☐	62:1—64:10 ☐	65:1—67:7 ☐	68:1-35 ☐	69:1—70:5 ☐	71:1—72:20 ☐	73:1—74:23 ☐
64	75:1—77:20 ☐	78:1-72 ☐	79:1—81:16 ☐	82:1—84:12 ☐	85:1—87:7 ☐	88:1—89:52 ☐	90:1—91:16 ☐
65	92:1—94:23 ☐	95:1—97:12 ☐	98:1—101:8 ☐	102:1—103:22 ☐	104:1—105:45 ☐	106:1-48 ☐	107:1-43 ☐
66	108:1—109:31 ☐	110:1—112:10 ☐	113:1—115:18 ☐	116:1—118:29 ☐	119:1-32 ☐	119:33-72 ☐	119:73-120 ☐
67	119:121-176 ☐	120:1—124:8 ☐	125:1—128:6 ☐	129:1—132:18 ☐	133:1—135:21 ☐	136:1—138:8 ☐	139:1—140:13 ☐
68	141:1—144:15 ☐	145:1—147:20 ☐	148:1—150:6 ☐	Prov. 1:1-33 ☐	2:1—3:35 ☐	4:1—5:23 ☐	6:1-35 ☐
69	7:1—8:36 ☐	9:1—10:32 ☐	11:1—12:28 ☐	13:1—14:35 ☐	15:1-33 ☐	16:1-33 ☐	17:1-28 ☐
70	18:1-24 ☐	19:1—20:30 ☐	21:1—22:29 ☐	23:1-35 ☐	24:1—25:28 ☐	26:1—27:27 ☐	28:1—29:27 ☐
71	30:1-33 ☐	31:1-31 ☐	Eccl. 1:1-18 ☐	2:1—3:22 ☐	4:1—5:20 ☐	6:1—7:29 ☐	8:1—9:18 ☐
72	10:1—11:10 ☐	12:1-14 ☐	S.S. 1:1-8 ☐	1:9-17 ☐	2:1-17 ☐	3:1-11 ☐	4:1-8 ☐
73	4:9-16 ☐	5:1-16 ☐	6:1-13 ☐	7:1-13 ☐	8:1-14 ☐	Isa. 1:1-11 ☐	1:12-31 ☐
74	2:1-22 ☐	3:1-26 ☐	4:1-6 ☐	5:1-30 ☐	6:1-13 ☐	7:1-25 ☐	8:1-22 ☐
75	9:1-21 ☐	10:1-34 ☐	11:1—12:6 ☐	13:1-22 ☐	14:1-14 ☐	14:15-32 ☐	15:1—16:14 ☐
76	17:1—18:7 ☐	19:1-25 ☐	20:1—21:17 ☐	22:1-25 ☐	23:1-18 ☐	24:1-23 ☐	25:1-12 ☐
77	26:1-21 ☐	27:1-13 ☐	28:1-29 ☐	29:1-24 ☐	30:1-33 ☐	31:1—32:20 ☐	33:1-24 ☐
78	34:1-17 ☐	35:1-10 ☐	36:1-22 ☐	37:1-38 ☐	38:1—39:8 ☐	40:1-31 ☐	41:1-29 ☐

Reading Schedule for the Recovery Version of the Old Testament with Footnotes

Wk.	Lord's Day	Monday	Tuesday	Wednesday	Thursday	Friday	Saturday
79	42:1-25 ☐	43:1-28 ☐	44:1-28 ☐	45:1-25 ☐	46:1-13 ☐	47:1-15 ☐	48:1-22 ☐
80	49:1-13 ☐	49:14-26 ☐	50:1—51:23 ☐	52:1-15 ☐	53:1-12 ☐	54:1-17 ☐	55:1-13 ☐
81	56:1-12 ☐	57:1-21 ☐	58:1-14 ☐	59:1-21 ☐	60:1-22 ☐	61:1-11 ☐	62:1-12 ☐
82	63:1-19 ☐	64:1-12 ☐	65:1-25 ☐	66:1-24 ☐	Jer. 1:1-19 ☐	2:1-19 ☐	2:20-37 ☐
83	3:1-25 ☐	4:1-31 ☐	5:1-31 ☐	6:1-30 ☐	7:1-34 ☐	8:1-22 ☐	9:1-26 ☐
84	10:1-25 ☐	11:1—12:17 ☐	13:1-27 ☐	14:1-22 ☐	15:1-21 ☐	16:1—17:27 ☐	18:1-23 ☐
85	19:1—20:18 ☐	21:1—22:30 ☐	23:1-40 ☐	24:1—25:38 ☐	26:1—27:22 ☐	28:1—29:32 ☐	30:1-24 ☐
86	31:1-23 ☐	31:24-40 ☐	32:1-44 ☐	33:1-26 ☐	34:1-22 ☐	35:1-19 ☐	36:1-32 ☐
87	37:1-21 ☐	38:1-28 ☐	39:1—40:16 ☐	41:1—42:22 ☐	43:1—44:30 ☐	45:1—46:28 ☐	47:1—48:16 ☐
88	48:17-47 ☐	49:1-22 ☐	49:23-39 ☐	50:1-27 ☐	50:28-46 ☐	51:1-27 ☐	51:28-64 ☐
89	52:1-34 ☐	Lam. 1:1-22 ☐	2:1-22 ☐	3:1-39 ☐	3:40-66 ☐	4:1-22 ☐	5:1-22 ☐
90	Ezek. 1:1-14 ☐	1:15-28 ☐	2:1—3:27 ☐	4:1—5:17 ☐	6:1—7:27 ☐	8:1—9:11 ☐	10:1—11:25 ☐
91	12:1—13:23 ☐	14:1—15:8 ☐	16:1-63 ☐	17:1—18:32 ☐	19:1-14 ☐	20:1-49 ☐	21:1-32 ☐
92	22:1-31 ☐	23:1-49 ☐	24:1-27 ☐	25:1—26:21 ☐	27:1-36 ☐	28:1-26 ☐	29:1—30:26 ☐
93	31:1—32:32 ☐	33:1-33 ☐	34:1-31 ☐	35:1—36:21 ☐	36:22-38 ☐	37:1-28 ☐	38:1—39:29 ☐
94	40:1-27 ☐	40:28-49 ☐	41:1-26 ☐	42:1—43:27 ☐	44:1-31 ☐	45:1-25 ☐	46:1-24 ☐
95	47:1-23 ☐	48:1-35 ☐	Dan. 1:1-21 ☐	2:1-30 ☐	2:31-49 ☐	3:1-30 ☐	4:1-37 ☐
96	5:1-31 ☐	6:1-28 ☐	7:1-12 ☐	7:13-28 ☐	8:1-27 ☐	9:1-27 ☐	10:1-21 ☐
97	11:1-22 ☐	11:23-45 ☐	12:1-13 ☐	Hosea 1:1-11 ☐	2:1-23 ☐	3:1—4:19 ☐	5:1-15 ☐
98	6:1-11 ☐	7:1-16 ☐	8:1-14 ☐	9:1-17 ☐	10:1-15 ☐	11:1-12 ☐	12:1-14 ☐
99	13:1—14:9 ☐	Joel 1:1-20 ☐	2:1-16 ☐	2:17-32 ☐	3:1-21 ☐	Amos 1:1-15 ☐	2:1-16 ☐
100	3:1-15 ☐	4:1—5:27 ☐	6:1—7:17 ☐	8:1—9:15 ☐	Obad. 1-21 ☐	Jonah 1:1-17 ☐	2:1—4:11 ☐
101	Micah 1:1-16 ☐	2:1—3:12 ☐	4:1—5:15 ☐	6:1—7:20 ☐	Nahum 1:1-15 ☐	1:1—3:19 ☐	Hab. 1:1-17 ☐
102	2:1-20 ☐	3:1-19 ☐	Zeph. 1:1-18 ☐	2:1-15 ☐	3:1-20 ☐	Hag. 1:1-15 ☐	2:1-23 ☐
103	Zech. 1:1-21 ☐	2:1-13 ☐	3:1-10 ☐	4:1-14 ☐	5:1—6:15 ☐	7:1—8:23 ☐	9:1-17 ☐
104	10:1—11:17 ☐	12:1—13:9 ☐	14:1-21 ☐	Mal. 1:1-14 ☐	2:1-17 ☐	3:1-18 ☐	4:1-6 ☐

Reading Schedule for the Recovery Version of the New Testament with Footnotes

Wk.	Lord's Day	Monday	Tuesday	Wednesday	Thursday	Friday	Saturday
1	Matt. 1:1-2 ☐	1:3-7 ☐	1:8-17 ☐	1:18-25 ☐	2:1-23 ☐	3:1-6 ☐	3:7-17 ☐
2	4:1-11 ☐	4:12-25 ☐	5:1-4 ☐	5:5-12 ☐	5:13-20 ☐	5:21-26 ☐	5:27-48 ☐
3	6:1-8 ☐	6:9-18 ☐	6:19-34 ☐	7:1-12 ☐	7:13-29 ☐	8:1-13 ☐	8:14-22 ☐
4	8:23-34 ☐	9:1-13 ☐	9:14-17 ☐	9:18-34 ☐	9:35—10:5 ☐	10:6-25 ☐	10:26-42 ☐
5	11:1-15 ☐	11:16-30 ☐	12:1-14 ☐	12:15-32 ☐	12:33-42 ☐	12:43—13:2 ☐	13:3-12 ☐
6	13:13-30 ☐	13:31-43 ☐	13:44-58 ☐	14:1-13 ☐	14:14-21 ☐	14:22-36 ☐	15:1-20 ☐
7	15:21-31 ☐	15:32-39 ☐	16:1-12 ☐	16:13-20 ☐	16:21-28 ☐	17:1-13 ☐	17:14-27 ☐
8	18:1-14 ☐	18:15-22 ☐	18:23-35 ☐	19:1-15 ☐	19:16-30 ☐	20:1-16 ☐	20:17-34 ☐
9	21:1-11 ☐	21:12-22 ☐	21:23-32 ☐	21:33-46 ☐	22:1-22 ☐	22:23-33 ☐	22:34-46 ☐
10	23:1-12 ☐	23:13-39 ☐	24:1-14 ☐	24:15-31 ☐	24:32-51 ☐	25:1-13 ☐	25:14-30 ☐
11	25:31-46 ☐	26:1-16 ☐	26:17-35 ☐	26:36-46 ☐	26:47-64 ☐	26:65-75 ☐	27:1-26 ☐
12	27:27-44 ☐	27:45-56 ☐	27:57—28:15 ☐	28:16-20 ☐	Mark 1:1 ☐	1:2-6 ☐	1:7-13 ☐
13	1:14-28 ☐	1:29-45 ☐	2:1-12 ☐	2:13-28 ☐	3:1-19 ☐	3:20-35 ☐	4:1-25 ☐
14	4:26-41 ☐	5:1-20 ☐	5:21-43 ☐	6:1-29 ☐	6:30-56 ☐	7:1-23 ☐	7:24-37 ☐
15	8:1-26 ☐	8:27—9:1 ☐	9:2-29 ☐	9:30-50 ☐	10:1-16 ☐	10:17-34 ☐	10:35-52 ☐
16	11:1-16 ☐	11:17-33 ☐	12:1-27 ☐	12:28-44 ☐	13:1-13 ☐	13:14-37 ☐	14:1-26 ☐
17	14:27-52 ☐	14:53-72 ☐	15:1-15 ☐	15:16-47 ☐	16:1-8 ☐	16:9-20 ☐	Luke 1:1-4 ☐
18	1:5-25 ☐	1:26-46 ☐	1:47-56 ☐	1:57-80 ☐	2:1-8 ☐	2:9-20 ☐	2:21-39 ☐
19	2:40-52 ☐	3:1-20 ☐	3:21-38 ☐	4:1-13 ☐	4:14-30 ☐	4:31-44 ☐	5:1-26 ☐
20	5:27—6:16 ☐	6:17-38 ☐	6:39-49 ☐	7:1-17 ☐	7:18-23 ☐	7:24-35 ☐	7:36-50 ☐
21	8:1-15 ☐	8:16-25 ☐	8:26-39 ☐	8:40-56 ☐	9:1-17 ☐	9:18-26 ☐	9:27-36 ☐
22	9:37-50 ☐	9:51-62 ☐	10:1-11 ☐	10:12-24 ☐	10:25-37 ☐	10:38-42 ☐	11:1-13 ☐
23	11:14-26 ☐	11:27-36 ☐	11:37-54 ☐	12:1-12 ☐	12:13-21 ☐	12:22-34 ☐	12:35-48 ☐
24	12:49-59 ☐	13:1-9 ☐	13:10-17 ☐	13:18-30 ☐	13:31—14:6 ☐	14:7-14 ☐	14:15-24 ☐
25	14:25-35 ☐	15:1-10 ☐	15:11-21 ☐	15:22-32 ☐	16:1-13 ☐	16:14-22 ☐	16:23-31 ☐
26	17:1-19 ☐	17:20-37 ☐	18:1-14 ☐	18:15-30 ☐	18:31-43 ☐	19:1-10 ☐	19:11-27 ☐

Reading Schedule for the Recovery Version of the New Testament with Footnotes

Wk.	Lord's Day	Monday	Tuesday	Wednesday	Thursday	Friday	Saturday
27	Luke 19:28-48 ☐	20:1-19 ☐	20:20-38 ☐	20:39—21:4 ☐	21:5-27 ☐	21:28-38 ☐	22:1-20 ☐
28	22:21-38 ☐	22:39-54 ☐	22:55-71 ☐	23:1-43 ☐	23:44-56 ☐	24:1-12 ☐	24:13-35 ☐
29	24:36-53 ☐	John 1:1-13 ☐	1:14-18 ☐	1:19-34 ☐	1:35-51 ☐	2:1-11 ☐	2:12-22 ☐
30	2:23—3:13 ☐	3:14-21 ☐	3:22-36 ☐	4:1-14 ☐	4:15-26 ☐	4:27-42 ☐	4:43-54 ☐
31	5:1-16 ☐	5:17-30 ☐	5:31-47 ☐	6:1-15 ☐	6:16-31 ☐	6:32-51 ☐	6:52-71 ☐
32	7:1-9 ☐	7:10-24 ☐	7:25-36 ☐	7:37-52 ☐	7:53—8:11 ☐	8:12-27 ☐	8:28-44 ☐
33	8:45-59 ☐	9:1-13 ☐	9:14-34 ☐	9:35—10:9 ☐	10:10-30 ☐	10:31—11:4 ☐	11:5-22 ☐
34	11:23-40 ☐	11:41-57 ☐	12:1-11 ☐	12:12-24 ☐	12:25-36 ☐	12:37-50 ☐	13:1-11 ☐
35	13:12-30 ☐	13:31-38 ☐	14:1-6 ☐	14:7-20 ☐	14:21-31 ☐	15:1-11 ☐	15:12-27 ☐
36	16:1-15 ☐	16:16-33 ☐	17:1-5 ☐	17:6-13 ☐	17:14-24 ☐	17:25—18:11 ☐	18:12-27 ☐
37	18:28-40 ☐	19:1-16 ☐	19:17-30 ☐	19:31-42 ☐	20:1-13 ☐	20:14-18 ☐	20:19-22 ☐
38	20:23-31 ☐	21:1-14 ☐	21:15-22 ☐	21:23-25 ☐	Acts 1:1-8 ☐	1:9-14 ☐	1:15-26 ☐
39	2:1-13 ☐	2:14-21 ☐	2:22-36 ☐	2:37-41 ☐	2:42-47 ☐	3:1-18 ☐	3:19—4:22 ☐
40	4:23-37 ☐	5:1-16 ☐	5:17-32 ☐	5:33-42 ☐	6:1—7:1 ☐	7:2-29 ☐	7:30-60 ☐
41	8:1-13 ☐	8:14-25 ☐	8:26-40 ☐	9:1-19 ☐	9:20-43 ☐	10:1-16 ☐	10:17-33 ☐
42	10:34-48 ☐	11:1-18 ☐	11:19-30 ☐	12:1-25 ☐	13:1-12 ☐	13:13-43 ☐	13:44—14:5 ☐
43	14:6-28 ☐	15:1-12 ☐	15:13-34 ☐	15:35—16:5 ☐	16:6-18 ☐	16:19-40 ☐	17:1-18 ☐
44	17:19-34 ☐	18:1-17 ☐	18:18-28 ☐	19:1-20 ☐	19:21-41 ☐	20:1-12 ☐	20:13-38 ☐
45	21:1-14 ☐	21:15-26 ☐	21:27-40 ☐	22:1-21 ☐	22:22-29 ☐	22:30—23:11 ☐	23:12-15 ☐
46	23:16-30 ☐	23:31—24:21 ☐	24:22—25:5 ☐	25:6-27 ☐	26:1-13 ☐	26:14-32 ☐	27:1-26 ☐
47	27:27—28:10 ☐	28:11-22 ☐	28:23-31 ☐	Rom. 1:1-2 ☐	1:3-7 ☐	1:8-17 ☐	1:18-25 ☐
48	1:26—2:10 ☐	2:11-29 ☐	3:1-20 ☐	3:21-31 ☐	4:1-12 ☐	4:13-25 ☐	5:1-11 ☐
49	5:12-17 ☐	5:18—6:5 ☐	6:6-11 ☐	6:12-23 ☐	7:1-12 ☐	7:13-25 ☐	8:1-2 ☐
50	8:3-6 ☐	8:7-13 ☐	8:14-25 ☐	8:26-39 ☐	9:1-18 ☐	9:19—10:3 ☐	10:4-15 ☐
51	10:16—11:10 ☐	11:11-22 ☐	11:23-36 ☐	12:1-3 ☐	12:4-21 ☐	13:1-14 ☐	14:1-12 ☐
52	14:13-23 ☐	15:1-13 ☐	15:14-33 ☐	16:1-5 ☐	16:6-24 ☐	16:25-27 ☐	1 Cor. 1:1-4 ☐

Reading Schedule for the Recovery Version of the New Testament with Footnotes

Wk.	Lord's Day	Monday	Tuesday	Wednesday	Thursday	Friday	Saturday
53	1 Cor. 1:5-9 ☐	1:10-17 ☐	1:18-31 ☐	2:1-5 ☐	2:6-10 ☐	2:11-16 ☐	3:1-9 ☐
54	3:10-13 ☐	3:14-23 ☐	4:1-9 ☐	4:10-21 ☐	5:1-13 ☐	6:1-11 ☐	6:12-20 ☐
55	7:1-16 ☐	7:17-24 ☐	7:25-40 ☐	8:1-13 ☐	9:1-15 ☐	9:16-27 ☐	10:1-4 ☐
56	10:5-13 ☐	10:14-33 ☐	11:1-6 ☐	11:7-16 ☐	11:17-26 ☐	11:27-34 ☐	12:1-11 ☐
57	12:12-22 ☐	12:23-31 ☐	13:1-13 ☐	14:1-12 ☐	14:13-25 ☐	14:26-33 ☐	14:34-40 ☐
58	15:1-19 ☐	15:20-28 ☐	15:29-34 ☐	15:35-49 ☐	15:50-58 ☐	16:1-9 ☐	16:10-24 ☐
59	2 Cor. 1:1-4 ☐	1:5-14 ☐	1:15-22 ☐	1:23—2:11 ☐	2:12-17 ☐	3:1-6 ☐	3:7-11 ☐
60	3:12-18 ☐	4:1-6 ☐	4:7-12 ☐	4:13-18 ☐	5:1-8 ☐	5:9-15 ☐	5:16-21 ☐
61	6:1-13 ☐	6:14—7:4 ☐	7:5-16 ☐	8:1-15 ☐	8:16-24 ☐	9:1-15 ☐	10:1-6 ☐
62	10:7-18 ☐	11:1-15 ☐	11:16-33 ☐	12:1-10 ☐	12:11-21 ☐	13:1-10 ☐	13:11-14 ☐
63	Gal. 1:1-5 ☐	1:6-14 ☐	1:15-24 ☐	2:1-13 ☐	2:14-21 ☐	3:1-4 ☐	3:5-14 ☐
64	3:15-22 ☐	3:23-29 ☐	4:1-7 ☐	4:8-20 ☐	4:21-31 ☐	5:1-12 ☐	5:13-21 ☐
65	5:22-26 ☐	6:1-10 ☐	6:11-15 ☐	6:16-18 ☐	Eph. 1:1-3 ☐	1:4-6 ☐	1:7-10 ☐
66	1:11-14 ☐	1:15-18 ☐	1:19-23 ☐	2:1-5 ☐	2:6-10 ☐	2:11-14 ☐	2:15-18 ☐
67	2:19-22 ☐	3:1-7 ☐	3:8-13 ☐	3:14-18 ☐	3:19-21 ☐	4:1-4 ☐	4:5-10 ☐
68	4:11-16 ☐	4:17-24 ☐	4:25-32 ☐	5:1-10 ☐	5:11-21 ☐	5:22-26 ☐	5:27-33 ☐
69	6:1-9 ☐	6:10-14 ☐	6:15-18 ☐	6:19-24 ☐	Phil. 1:1-7 ☐	1:8-18 ☐	1:19-26 ☐
70	1:27—2:4 ☐	2:5-11 ☐	2:12-16 ☐	2:17-30 ☐	3:1-6 ☐	3:7-11 ☐	3:12-16 ☐
71	3:17-21 ☐	4:1-9 ☐	4:10-23 ☐	Col. 1:1-8 ☐	1:9-13 ☐	1:14-23 ☐	1:24-29 ☐
72	2:1-7 ☐	2:8-15 ☐	2:16-23 ☐	3:1-4 ☐	3:5-15 ☐	3:16-25 ☐	4:1-18 ☐
73	1 Thes. 1:1-3 ☐	1:4-10 ☐	2:1-12 ☐	2:13—3:5 ☐	3:6-13 ☐	4:1-10 ☐	4:11—5:11 ☐
74	5:12-28 ☐	2 Thes. 1:1-12 ☐	2:1-17 ☐	3:1-18 ☐	1 Tim. 1:1-2 ☐	1:3-4 ☐	1:5-14 ☐
75	1:15-20 ☐	2:1-7 ☐	2:8-15 ☐	3:1-13 ☐	3:14—4:5 ☐	4:6-16 ☐	5:1-25 ☐
76	6:1-10 ☐	6:11-21 ☐	2 Tim. 1:1-10 ☐	1:11-18 ☐	2:1-15 ☐	2:16-26 ☐	3:1-13 ☐
77	3:14—4:8 ☐	4:9-22 ☐	Titus 1:1-4 ☐	1:5-16 ☐	2:1-15 ☐	3:1-8 ☐	3:9-15 ☐
78	Philem. 1:1-11 ☐	1:12-25 ☐	Heb. 1:1-2 ☐	1:3-5 ☐	1:6-14 ☐	2:1-9 ☐	2:10-18 ☐

Reading Schedule for the Recovery Version of the New Testament with Footnotes

Wk.	Lord's Day	Monday	Tuesday	Wednesday	Thursday	Friday	Saturday
79	Heb. 3:1-6 □	3:7-19 □	4:1-9 □	4:10-13 □	4:14-16 □	5:1-10 □	5:11—6:3 □
80	6:4-8 □	6:9-20 □	7:1-10 □	7:11-28 □	8:1-6 □	8:7-13 □	9:1-4 □
81	9:5-14 □	9:15-28 □	10:1-18 □	10:19-28 □	10:29-39 □	11:1-6 □	11:7-19 □
82	11:20-31 □	11:32-40 □	12:1-2 □	12:3-13 □	12:14-17 □	12:18-26 □	12:27-29 □
83	13:1-7 □	13:8-12 □	13:13-15 □	13:16-25 □	James 1:1-8 □	1:9-18 □	1:19-27 □
84	2:1-13 □	2:14-26 □	3:1-18 □	4:1-10 □	4:11-17 □	5:1-12 □	5:13-20 □
85	1 Pet. 1:1-2 □	1:3-4 □	1:5 □	1:6-9 □	1:10-12 □	1:13-17 □	1:18-25 □
86	2:1-3 □	2:4-8 □	2:9-17 □	2:18-25 □	3:1-13 □	3:14-22 □	4:1-6 □
87	4:7-16 □	4:17-19 □	5:1-4 □	5:5-9 □	5:10-14 □	2 Pet. 1:1-2 □	1:3-4 □
88	1:5-8 □	1:9-11 □	1:12-18 □	1:19-21 □	2:1-3 □	2:4-11 □	2:12-22 □
89	3:1-6 □	3:7-9 □	3:10-12 □	3:13-15 □	3:16 □	3:17-18 □	1 John 1:1-2 □
90	1:3-4 □	1:5 □	1:6 □	1:7 □	1:8-10 □	2:1-2 □	2:3-11 □
91	2:12-14 □	2:15-19 □	2:20-23 □	2:24-27 □	2:28-29 □	3:1-5 □	3:6-10 □
92	3:11-18 □	3:19-24 □	4:1-6 □	4:7-11 □	4:12-15 □	4:16—5:3 □	5:4-13 □
93	5:14-17 □	5:18-21 □	2 John 1:1-3 □	1:4-9 □	1:10-13 □	3 John 1:1-6 □	1:7-14 □
94	Jude 1:1-4 □	1:5-10 □	1:11-19 □	1:20-25 □	Rev. 1:1-3 □	1:4-6 □	1:7-11 □
95	1:12-13 □	1:14-16 □	1:17-20 □	2:1-6 □	2:7 □	2:8-9 □	2:10-11 □
96	2:12-14 □	2:15-17 □	2:18-23 □	2:24-29 □	3:1-3 □	3:4-6 □	3:7-9 □
97	3:10-13 □	3:14-18 □	3:19-22 □	4:1-5 □	4:6-7 □	4:8-11 □	5:1-6 □
98	5:7-14 □	6:1-8 □	6:9-17 □	7:1-8 □	7:9-17 □	8:1-6 □	8:7-12 □
99	8:13—9:11 □	9:12-21 □	10:1-4 □	10:5-11 □	11:1-4 □	11:5-14 □	11:15-19 □
100	12:1-4 □	12:5-9 □	12:10-18 □	13:1-10 □	13:11-18 □	14:1-5 □	14:6-12 □
101	14:13-20 □	15:1-8 □	16:1-12 □	16:13-21 □	17:1-6 □	17:7-18 □	18:1-8 □
102	18:9—19:4 □	19:5-10 □	19:11-16 □	19:17-21 □	20:1-6 □	20:7-10 □	20:11-15 □
103	21:1 □	21:2 □	21:3-8 □	21:9-13 □	21:14-18 □	21:19-21 □	21:22-27 □
104	22:1 □	22:2 □	22:3-11 □	22:12-15 □	22:16-17 □	22:18-21 □	

Week 1 — Day 4   Today's verses

Gen. 2:10 And a river went forth from Eden to water the garden, and from there it divided and became four branches.

Rev. 22:1 And he showed me a river of water of life, bright as crystal, proceeding out of the throne of God and of the Lamb in the middle of its street.

_____
Date

Week 1 — Day 5   Today's verses

Gen. 2:11-12 The name of the first [branch] is Pishon; it is the one that goes around the whole land of Havilah, where there is gold. And the gold of that land is good; bdellium and onyx stone are there.

Rev. 21:18 And the building work of its wall was jasper; and the city was pure gold, like clear glass.

21 And the twelve gates were twelve pearls; each one of the gates was, respectively, of one pearl...

_____
Date

Week 1 — Day 6   Today's verses

Gen. 2:22 And Jehovah God built the rib, which He had taken from the man, into a woman and brought her to the man.

Eph. 5:25-27 Husbands, love your wives even as Christ also loved the church and gave Himself up for her that He might sanctify her, cleansing her by the washing of the water in the word, that He might present the church to Himself glorious...

_____
Date

Week 1 — Day 1   Today's verses

Gen. 1:26 And God said, Let Us make man in Our image, according to Our likeness...and let them have dominion...over all the earth...

2:9 And out of the ground Jehovah God caused to grow every tree that is pleasant to the sight and good for food, as well as the tree of life in the middle of the garden and the tree of the knowledge of good and evil.

_____
Date

Week 1 — Day 2   Today's verses

Gen. 2:22 ...Jehovah God built the rib, which He had taken from the man, into a woman and brought her to the man.

Rev. 22:17 And the Spirit and the bride say, Come! And let him who hears say, Come! And let him who is thirsty come; let him who wills take the water of life freely.

_____
Date

Week 1 — Day 3   Today's verses

John 14:6 Jesus said... I am the way and the reality and the life; no one comes to the Father except through Me.

15:1 I am the true vine, and My Father is the husbandman.

Rev. 22:14 Blessed are those who wash their robes that they may have right to the tree of life and may enter by the gates into the city.

_____
Date

Week 2 — Day 6 — Today's verses

Col. 1:15 Who is the image of the invisible God, the Firstborn of all creation.

18 And He is the Head of the Body, the church; He is the beginning, the Firstborn from the dead, that He Himself might have the first place in all things.

Week 2 — Day 3 — Today's verses

Col. 1:9 ...That you may be filled with the full knowledge of His will in all spiritual wisdom and understanding.

Eph. 1:5 Predestinating us unto sonship through Jesus Christ to Himself, according to the good pleasure of His will.

11 In whom also we were designated as an inheritance, having been predestinated according to the purpose of the One who works all things according to the counsel of His will.

Week 2 — Day 5 — Today's verses

Col. 1:16-17 Because in Him all things were created, in the heavens and on the earth, the visible and the invisible, whether thrones or lordships or rulers or authorities; all things have been created through Him and unto Him. And He is before all things, and all things cohere in Him.

Week 2 — Day 2 — Today's verses

Eph. 1:9 Making known to us the mystery of His will according to His good pleasure, which He purposed in Himself.

Rev. 4:11 You are worthy, our Lord and God, to receive the glory and the honor and the power, for You have created all things, and because of Your will they were, and were created.

Week 2 — Day 4 — Today's verses

John 1:3 All things came into being through Him, and apart from Him not one thing came into being which has come into being.

Heb. 1:10 And, "You in the beginning, Lord, laid the foundation of the earth, and the heavens are the works of Your hands."

Week 2 — Day 1 — Today's verses

Gen. 1:1 In the beginning God created the heavens and the earth.

Eph. 3:9 And to enlighten all *that they may see what the* economy of the mystery is, which throughout the ages has been hidden in God, who created all things.

Week 3 — Day 4   Today's verses

Gen. ...God said, Let there be light-bearers in the
1:14-16 expanse of heaven to separate the day from the night, and let them be for signs and for seasons and for days and years...and let them be...to give light on the earth; and it was so. And God made the two great light-bearers, the greater light-bearer to rule the day and the lesser light-bearer to rule the night, and the stars.

Date _____

Week 3 — Day 5   Today's verses

Gen. And God said, Let the waters swarm with
1:20-21 swarms of living animals, and let birds fly above the earth in the open expanse of heaven. And God created the great sea creatures and every living animal that moves, with which the waters swarmed, according to their kind, and every winged bird according to its kind; and God saw that it was good.

Date _____

Week 3 — Day 6   Today's verses

Gen. And God said, Let the earth bring forth liv-
1:24 ing animals according to their kind, cattle and creeping things and animals of the earth...and it was so.

26 And God said, Let Us make man in Our image, according to Our likeness; and let them have dominion over the fish of the sea and over the birds of heaven and over the cattle and over all the earth and over every creeping thing that creeps upon the earth.

Date _____

Week 3 — Day 1   Today's verses

Gen. But the earth became waste and empti-
1:2-4 ness, and darkness was on the surface of the deep, and the Spirit of God was brooding upon the surface of the waters. And God said, Let there be light; and there was light. And God saw that the light was good, and God separated the light from the darkness.

Date _____

Week 3 — Day 2   Today's verses

Gen. And God made the expanse and sepa-
1:7-9 rated the waters which were under the expanse from the waters which were above the expanse, and it was so. And God called the expanse Heaven. And there was evening and there was morning, a second day. And God said, Let the waters under the heavens be gathered together into one place, and let the dry land appear; and it was so.

Date _____

Week 3 — Day 3   Today's verses

Gen. And God called the dry land Earth, and
1:10-11 the gathering together of the waters He called Seas; and God saw that it was good. And God said, Let the earth sprout grass, herbs yielding seed, and fruit trees bearing fruit according to their kind with their seed in them upon the earth; and it was so.

Date _____

Week 4 — Day 6 — Today's verses

Rev. 4:3 And He who was sitting was like a jasper stone and a sardius in appearance, and *there was* a rainbow around the throne like an emerald in appearance.

21:11 Having the glory of God. Her light was like a most precious stone, like a jasper stone, as clear as crystal.

_____
Date

Week 4 — Day 5 — Today's verses

Luke 1:31-32 And behold, you will conceive in *your* womb and bear a son, and you shall call His name Jesus. He will be great and will be called Son of the Most High....

Rom. 5:10 For if we, being enemies, were reconciled to God through the death of His Son, much more we will be saved in His life, having been reconciled.

_____
Date

Week 4 — Day 4 — Today's verses

1 Cor. 15:45 So also it is written, "The first man, Adam, became a living soul"; the last Adam *became* a life-giving Spirit.

Col. 1:15 Who is the image of the invisible God, the Firstborn of all creation.

_____
Date

Week 4 — Day 3 — Today's verses

John 12:24 Truly, truly, I say to you, Unless the grain of wheat falls into the ground and dies, it abides alone; but if it dies, it bears much fruit.

Rom. 8:29 Because those whom He foreknew, He also predestinated *to be* conformed to the image of His Son, that He might be the First-born among many brothers.

_____
Date

Week 4 — Day 2 — Today's verses

Eph. 3:17 That Christ may make His home in your hearts through faith....

2 Cor. 3:18 But we all with unveiled face, beholding and reflecting like a mirror the glory of the Lord, are being transformed into the same image from glory to glory, even as from the Lord Spirit.

_____
Date

Week 4 — Day 1 — Today's verses

Gen. 1:26-27 And God said, Let Us make man in Our image, according to Our likeness; and let them have dominion over the fish of the sea and over the birds of heaven and over the cattle and over all the earth and over every creeping thing that creeps upon the earth. And God created man in His own image; in the image of God He created him; male and female He created them.

_____
Date

Week 5 — Day 1

Today's verses

Gen. And God said, Let Us make man in Our im-
1:26 age, according to Our likeness; and let
them have dominion over the fish of the sea
and over the birds of heaven and over the
cattle and over all the earth and over every
creeping thing that creeps upon the earth.

28 And God blessed them; and God said to
them, Be fruitful and multiply, and fill the
earth and subdue it, and have dominion...

Week 5 — Day 2

Today's verses

Psa. O Jehovah our Lord, how excellent is Your
8:1-2 name in all the earth, You who have set
Your glory over the heavens! Out of the
mouths of babes and sucklings You have
established strength because of Your adver-
saries, to stop the enemy and the avenger.

Week 5 — Day 3

Today's verses

Matt. Your kingdom come; Your will be done, as
6:10 in heaven, so also on earth.

16:18-19 ...Upon this rock I will build My church,
and the gates of Hades shall not prevail
against it. I will give to you the keys of the
kingdom of the heavens, and whatever
you bind on the earth shall have been
bound in the heavens, and whatever you
loose on the earth shall have been loosed
in the heavens.

Week 5 — Day 4

Today's verses

Matt. And do not bring us into temptation, but
6:13 deliver us from the evil one. For Yours is
the kingdom and the power and the glory
forever. Amen.

1 Cor. The first man is out of the earth, earthy;
15:47 the second man is out of heaven.

Week 5 — Day 5

Today's verses

Rom. For just as through the disobedience of one
5:19 man the many were constituted sinners, so
also through the obedience of the One the
many will be constituted righteous.

Eph. Abolishing in His flesh the law of the
2:15 commandments in ordinances, that He
might create the two in Himself into one
new man, so making peace.

Week 5 — Day 6

Today's verses

Eph. And put on the new man, which was cre-
4:24 ated according to God in righteousness
and holiness of the reality.

Rev. And night will be no more; and they have
22:5 no need of the light of a lamp and of the
light of the sun, for the Lord God will
shine upon them; and they will reign forever and ever.

Week 6 — Day 1   Today's verses

Gen. And out of the ground Jehovah God caused
2:9 to grow every tree that is pleasant to the sight and good for food, as well as the tree of life in the middle of the garden and the tree of the knowledge of good and evil.

John I am the true vine, and My Father is the
15:1 husbandman.

6:48 I am the bread of life.

Date

Week 6 — Day 2   Today's verses

Gen. But of the tree of the knowledge of good
2:17 and evil, of it you shall not eat; for in the day that you eat of it you shall surely die.

2 Cor. Who has also made us sufficient as minis-
3:6 ters of a new covenant, *ministers* not of the letter but of the Spirit; for the letter kills, but the Spirit gives life.

Date

Week 6 — Day 3   Today's verses

Gen. And Jehovah God commanded the man,
2:16-17 saying, Of every tree of the garden you may eat freely, but of the tree of the knowledge of good and evil, of it you shall not eat; for in the day that you eat of it you shall surely die.

Eph. And you, though dead in your offenses
2:1 and sins.

Date

Week 6 — Day 4   Today's verses

John I am the vine; you are the branches. He
15:5 who abides in Me and I in him, he bears much fruit; for apart from Me you can do nothing.

Gen. For God knows that in the day you eat of it
3:5 your eyes will be opened, and you will become like God, knowing good and evil.

Date

Week 6 — Day 5   Today's verses

Gen. And Abel also brought an *offering*, from
4:4 the firstlings of his flock, that is, from their fat portions. And Jehovah had regard for Abel and for his offering.

5:24 And Enoch walked with God, and he was not, for God took him.

Date

Week 6 — Day 6   Today's verses

Exo. And He said, My presence shall go *with*
33:14 *you*, and I will give you rest.

John As the living Father has sent Me and I live
6:57 because of the Father, so he who eats Me, he also shall live because of Me.

Date